CONDITIONING FOR DISTANCE RUNNING

AMERICAN COLLEGE OF
SPORTS MEDICINE SERIES

CONDITIONING FOR DISTANCE RUNNING

JACK DANIELS
University of Texas-Austin

ROBERT FITTS
Marquette University

GEORGE SHEEHAN
Red Bank, New Jersey

JOHN WILEY & SONS
New York   Santa Barbara   Chichester   Brisbane   Toronto

Library of Congress Cataloging in Publication Data

Daniels, Jack, 1933-
    Conditioning for distance running.

    (American College of Sports Medicine series)
    1. Running–Physiological effect. 2. Running–Training.
I. Fitts, Robert, joint author. II. Sheehan, George, joint author.
III. Title. IV. Series.

RC1220.R8D36   613.7'1   77-22538
ISBN 0-471-19483-2

Printed in the United States of America

10 9 8 7 6 5 4 3 2 1

FOREWORD

During the past 10 years, a tremendous explosion of knowledge has occurred in the exercise and sport sciences. New theories in the coaching and training of athletes have emerged, technological breakthroughs have allowed a better understanding of how people perform and adapt to the stress of exercise, and we now have a better understanding as to how exercise can improve both the quality and quantity of life. In addition, the population of the United States has become more conscious of physical fitness and has started exercising on their own, with little or no knowledge of what to do or how to go about it. Consequently, many commerical enterprises have evolved to satisfy this basic consumer need. Although many of these enterprises have provided valuable consumer services, there are many others that have not had the consumer's best interests at heart and have taken advantage of the general lack of knowledge of the average consumer.

In 1973, the American College of Sports Medicine, at the suggestion of their former President, Dr. Howard G. Knuttgen, planned a series of volumes to help bridge the widening gap between the latest research in the exercise and sport sciences and the consumer. The purpose of this Series was to bring to the level of the average consumer, the facts and basic information related to exercise in general, and individual sports specifically, in an interesting and unbiased manner. Dr. David L. Costill, currently President of the American College of Sports Medicine, was asked to initiate this Series.

The American College of Sports Medicine's Series is an exciting step forward in the area of consumer education. Each volume is co-authored by authorities in their respective areas, who were selected for their ability to communicate their ideas at a very practical and fundamental level. While each of these authors is a recognized scientist, each volume represents an attempt to apply the teachings and findings of science to the better understanding of and participation in various activities and sports. It is the intent of this Series to develop a more informed consumer and to stimulate widespread participation in a variety of activities and sports.

JACK H. WILMORE
Chairperson, Publications Committee
American College of Sports Medicine

PREFACE

Our objective is to review the scientific knowledge pertinent to human performance and, particularly, to distance running. It is impossible to give a training prescription that fits all distance runners because the specifics of a program depend on each runner's weaknesses and strengths and the event for which each is training. However, the knowledge presented here will form the foundations on which each runner can develop his or her own ideal training program.

We begin by discussing the physiological systems that are of major importance in distance running—the neuromuscular, cardiovascular, and respiratory systems and their adaptation to endurance training. A detailed description of body metabolism, both oxidative (aerobic) and nonoxidative (anaerobic), is given. Then we consider environmental and nutritional factors. The section on training and running technique presents specific types of training that should be a part of every distance runner's program. The scientific rationale for the importance of the specific types of training is discussed. The most common injuries afflicting distance runners are described, and emphasis is placed on their prevention through daily stretching exercises. We conclude with a profile of the characteristics common to champion distance runners.

Keep in mind that many people run purely for enjoyment or fitness, with no intention of ever becoming competitive.

However, through greater participation, there will be a greater number of competitive distance runners. They come in all sizes, types, and ages, and proper knowledge can be gained and practiced only by an understanding of the basic systems involved and the principles on which reactions and adjustments to training and our environment are based.

Inaccuracies abound in athletics, and in an activity as popular and as potentially stressful as distance running, there is no room for mis-information directed toward either the jogger or the Olympic champion; both are equally deserving of proper guidance. We believe that this book contributes toward a better understanding of distance running.

JACK DANIELS

ROBERT FITTS

GEORGE SHEEHAN

CONTENTS

SECTION 1

Physiological and Biochemical Considerations

Endurance running places certain demands on the physiological systems of the body. In particular, running stresses the cardiovascular, respiratory, and neuromuscular systems. A hard, continuous run requires the heart to increase its minute output as much as fourfold, a requirement that it meets by increasing both the heart rate and the stroke volume (amount of blood pumped out of the heart with each beat). The respiratory system increases its air movement by an even greater magnitude by increasing both the volume of each breath and the frequency of breaths per minute. The neuromuscular system, especially the nerves and muscles of the legs, experiences perhaps the biggest stress during running. At rest, this system functions mainly as a stabilizer of the body position, a function maintained mainly by tonic contraction of particular muscle groups. During running, the muscles of the lower extremity not only stabilize but also move the body; this requires both rapid, forceful contractions (called phasic contraction) and slow, maintained contractions (called tonic contraction). Because of the importance of these three systems to distance running performance, their physiological and biochemical adaptions to endurance running will be discussed.

1

NEUROMUSCULAR SYSTEM

Movement depends on a coordinated interaction of the nervous and muscular systems. The major leg muscles responsible for locomotion in humans are composed of hundreds of muscle fibers, each innervated by a nerve. While a single muscle fiber is innervated by only one nerve ending, each nerve and its branches innervates from 10 to 200 or more muscle fibers. A motor unit is thus composed of a single nerve and all the muscle fibers that it innervates.

Human muscle has two distinct fiber types. One appears red because of a rich vascularization and myoglobin content (myoglobin is a protein that binds and transports oxygen across a muscle fiber in a manner similar to the role of hemoglobin in blood). This fiber is slow contracting and fatigue resistant, and hence it is designated a slow, red fiber. It contains a high content of mitochondria (the subcellular structures within muscle fibers where oxygen is consumed and energy is produced through a series of linked, chemical reactions). The high degree of vascularization, myoglobin, and mitochondrial content combine to give this type of fiber a high capacity to consume oxygen. This means of generating energy, by oxidative metabolism, is called aerobic metabolism – the process where the energy produced depends on an adequate supply of oxygen. The slow, red fiber is recruited for prolonged muscular work; hence, it is not suprising that the leg muscles of marathon runners contain a high percentage of these slow, *oxidative* fibers.

The second major fiber type in human muscle is fast contracting. It has two subdivisions that are generally described as fast, white and fast, red fibers. The fast, white fiber has a poor vascularization, low myoglobin and mitochondria content, and hence a poor capacity for the generation of energy through oxidative metabolism. The fast, white fiber is mainly used where a quick burst of muscle force is needed. Therefore, the leg muscles of a good sprinter contain a high percentage of this fiber type. The white fiber obtains its energy mainly by means of nonoxidative metabolism – through a series of chemical reactions that generate energy without requiring oxygen. This type of metabolism is called anaerobic metabolism. The general series of reactions involved are collectively called glycolysis, since the starting energy source is muscle glycogen or blood glucose. These carbohydrates are broken down (glycolized), producing energy and a metabolic end product called lactic acid. Glycolysis, anaerobic metabolism, provides a quick energy source, but cannot be maintained for prolonged periods, since a buildup in muscle lactic acid leads to muscle fatigue.

The fast, red fiber has a rich vascularization, a high myoglobin and mitochondrial content, and hence it has a high capacity for oxidative metabolism. This fiber type has a relatively high capacity for both aerobic and anaerobic metabolism and is, therefore, ideal for performing work of a high intensity and moderate duration. Although it has not been extensively studied, one would predict that middle distance runners (880—yard) would have a higher percentage of this fiber type in their leg muscles compared to either sprinters or marathon runners. Table 1 summarizes some of the characteristics of different types of muscle fibers.

TABLE 1. Characteristics of human skeletal and heart muscle fibers

| FIBER TYPE | VASCU-LARIZA-TION | CAPACITY FOR METABOLISM | | FATIGUE RESIST-ANCE |
		OXIDA-TIVE	NONOXI-DATIVE	
Slow, red	High	High	Low	High
Fast, white	Low	Low	High	Low
Fast, red	High	Moderate	High	Moderate
Heart muscle	High	High	Low	High

Although there are two general types of muscle fibers (fast and slow contracting), all fibers have the same anatomical arrangement of the basic muscle proteins (the main structural elements of all body organs are composed of proteins). Two important muscle proteins that allow for muscle shortening by interacting with each other are actin and myosin. The myosin protein has a specialized section that controls the rate at which the high energy molecules produced during either aerobic or anaerobic metabolism are split, and hence the rate at which energy is made available for muscle shortening. The high energy substance produced during metabolism is called adenosine triphosphate, abbreviated ATP. When this molecule is split, energy is made available for muscle contraction. The specialized section of the protein myosin that controls the rate at which ATP is split is called myosin ATPase. The myosin from fast-contracting fibers (fast, red and fast, white) contains a high level of myosin ATPase while the myosin of the slow, red fibers contains lower levels of myosin ATPase. Therefore, fast fibers when activated by their nerve, split ATP faster and contract faster than slow fibers.

Human muscle is generally heterogeneous, being composed of both fast- and slow-contracting muscle fibers. The antigravity muscles of the lower extremity (the extensor muscles that are closest to the bone) are tonically active, and hence the slow, red fibers predominate. The more superficial muscles are used less but in a quicker, more phasic action, and consequently they have a higher percentage of fast-contracting fibers than the deep, antigravity muscles.

Endurance training has been shown to increase the level of myosin ATPase in the slow, red fibers and decrease its level in the fast, red fibers of animals. No effect was observed on the fast, white fibers. The physiological significance of these measurements is not yet known. One can only speculate that if the biochemical changes observed have any physiological significance, then a slow, red fiber would be faster and a fast, red fiber slightly slower following an endurance running program. This type of training has no effect on the level of myosin ATPase measured in the fast, white fibers, probably because endurance running does not result in much recruitment of this fiber type.

It has been demonstrated in heterogenous muscles that an endurance running program (either continuous or intermittent running) will increase the muscles' resistance to fatigue. An isolated muscle from a trained animal maintains a higher percentage of its peak force during 45 minutes of electrical stimulation than does a similarly treated untrained muscle. It seems likely that trained muscles will not only fatigue less rapidly during prolonged stimulation, but they will contract and generate force more rapidly than an untrained muscle. These physiological adaptations to training need to be studied on homogeneous muscle (muscle made up predominantly of one fiber type) before the physiological effects of endurance running can be clearly understood.

As discussed previously, skeletal muscle has two main metabolic pathways for the generation of energy (ATP). The nonoxidative pathway, anaerobic metabolism, depends on carbohydrate (muscle glycogen and blood glucose). Lactic acid is an end product of this pathway. Because anaerobic metabolism cannot support work for extended periods, it is considered of little importance in distance running events. Often, however, it is reasonable to assume that although the total energy supplied by anaerobic means is low, relative to that supplied by oxidative metabolism in distance running, the anaerobic source is important during certain stages of the run. We will discuss this concept in Sections 2 and 5.

Endurance training has been shown to have little or no effect on the capacity of the different fiber types to generate energy by glycolysis (anaerobic metabolism). If there is a trend, it is toward a slight decrease in the capacity of this system. Exercise training of a shorter duration but higher intensity, which may be equated to repeat runs of from 440 yards to one mile in distance, has been shown to increase the capacity of the anaerobic system in slow, red fibers but to have no effect on fast-contracting fibers.

The main source of energy in endurance work is supplied by the oxidative- or aerobic-metabolic pathway. The fuel source may be either carbohydrate or fat, but generally both fuels are used in endurance running. From the standpoint of energy supplied, fat is quantitatively the most important fuel source in distance running. However, muscle glycogen and blood glucose are also very important for prolonged work of moderate intensity (such as competitive distance running where the top runners work at about 80 percent of their maximal oxidative work capacity for over two hours). Prolonged, light work (a load requiring less than 70 percent of an individual's maximal oxidative capacity) can be sustained almost entirely from the oxidative metabolism of fat. However, as the work load is increased toward an individual's maximal oxidative capacity, carbohydrate supplies a greater percent of the energy. Champion three- and six-milers perform at work loads that are approximately 95 percent of their maximal aerobic (oxidative) capacity while good marathon runners run at work loads that are over 80 percent of the maximal capacity. During such work loads, muscle glycogen is an important fuel. In fact, development of fatigue during prolonged running has been linked to muscle-glycogen depletion.

Regular endurance training has been shown to cause as much as a twofold increase in the concentration of specific enzymes within mitochondria that are involved in oxidative metabolism of both carbohydrate and fat. The size and number of mitochondria also increase in all fiber types as does the muscle myoglobin concentration. The muscle fibers themselves do not hypertrophy (enlarge in size) nor is the muscle weight to body weight ratio changed following endurance training (in contrast, a heavy overload stress such as weight lifting has been shown to result in muscle hypertrophy).

The degree of change in the number of mitochondria and the concentration increases of the proteins involved in aerobic metabolism are dependent on the duration of the training runs. Table 2 shows the increase observed in cytochrome c (a protein involved in oxidative metabolism and located in mitochondria) in rat muscle with different durations of daily training five days a week for 14 weeks.

TABLE 2. Changes in cytochrome c in rat muscle with different amounts of training

GROUPS	CYTOCHROME c, % INCREASE
Sedentary	0
10-Minute daily running	10
30-Minute daily running	30
60-Minute daily running	40
120-Minute daily running	100

In this experiment, the protein concentration increased as the duration of daily running increased. Running beyond two hours a day brings little further increase in mitochondrial protein, and generally results eventually in deterioration, as the animal becomes chronically fatigued and unable to complete the daily run. At the other extreme, a stress above some minimal level is required before muscle adaptation occurs. In the experiment reported in Table 2, 10 minutes a day, five days a week was adequate. However, another investigation found 30 minutes of daily swimming for eight weeks to have no effect. It is important to point out that this study was performed on rats. Completely untrained rats can swim for more than six hours, provided that the water is at the proper temperature. Therefore, it can be concluded that there is a minimal stress below which no effects will be observed and a maximal stress above which no further increases will occur. Actually, a reduction in adaptive changes may result because of chronic fatigue.

CARDIOVASCULAR SYSTEM

The cardiovascular system is made up of a central pump, which consists of the heart itself and the peripheral vasculature, including the arteries, capillaries, and veins.

The heart is a specialized type of muscle that functions as a pump and circulates oxygenated blood through the vascular system to the various organ systems of the body. Heart muscle contains certain structures found in all types of muscles, including the proteins that participate in shortening (called contractile proteins) and the proteins that function in the oxidative and nonoxidative metabolic pathways of energy generation. The main contractile proteins of heart muscle are the same as those of skeletal muscle, actin and myosin. Heart muscle has a rich supply of blood vessels, an extremely high mitochondrial content, and it is slow contracting. The myosin ATPase (the specialized part of the myosin molecule that controls the rate of ATP splitting and the speed of muscle shortening) concentration is slightly higher than that in slow, red skeletal muscle, but considerably lower than either type of fast skeletal muscle fiber. Due to the extremely high mitochondrial content, heart muscle has a very high capacity for oxidative metabolism. The nonoxidative metabolic capacity is low, and hence heart muscle needs a constant oxygen supply in order to produce the ATP needed to maintain its pumping action.

In contrast to skeletal muscle, heart muscle hypertrophies in response to a daily endurance running program. As a result, the heart weight to body weight ratio increases. Table 3 shows that as little as 10 minutes of running five days a week is enough to cause some heart muscle hypertrophy in rats, while the maximal effect is reached with 30 minutes of daily running.

Heart muscle is difficult to study physiologically, due to the anatomical arrangement of the muscle fibers and their physiological properties. The fibers are not aligned longitudinally, as in skeletal muscle, but branch out from each other forming a complicated meshwork. There are no discrete tendons to which force transducers can be tied, which makes force measurements difficult. Heart muscle cannot be tetanized (a sustained contraction of muscle resulting from multiple stimuli in rapid succession), since the fibers are insensitive to stimulation for a short period of time following an initial stimulus. This is function-

TABLE 3. Relative weights of rat hearts associated with different amounts of training

GROUPS	HEART WEIGHT/ BODY WEIGHT RATIO
Sedentary	2.40
10-minute daily running	2.65
30-minute daily running	2.80
60-minute daily running	2.75
120-minute daily running	2.81

ally important, because the heart could not act as a pump if it remained contracted — the pumping action depends on a rhythmic contraction and relaxation. Because of these technical difficulties, there have been few studies on the physiological adaptations of heart muscle to endurance running. The myosin ATPase content has been shown to increase slightly with training; hence, one would predict that the heart muscle fibers would contract faster after adapting to an endurance running program. Hearts from trained animals have been shown to contract with more force and to generate force faster than untrained controls. Human subjects have a lower resting heart rate (often 40 beats per minute or less) and lower maximal heart rates during maximal work, as a result of training. Despite a lower maximal heart rate, the trained individual can pump more blood per minute (higher cardiac output) than he or she could before training. The increase in flow per minute is obtained because the hypertrophied heart is able to pump out more blood per beat (higher stroke volume) without increasing the ejection time. The trained heart is thus more efficient, since it pumps more blood with fewer beats.

Although the maximal cardiac output is higher after training, the output during a set submaximal load is unchanged. The blood flow per kilogram-working muscle is actually slightly lower in the trained compared to the untrained state during submaximal work. The trained muscle compensates for slightly lower flow by increasing the amount of oxygen extracted from the blood as it passes through the muscle. Consequently, unless there is an improvement in technique and running efficiency, the oxygen consumed during submaximal work is not altered by training. The oxygen consumed is directly related to the intensity of the work. Of course, following a training program, an individual has a greater maximal oxygen consumption (the body's maximum capacity for consuming oxygen and providing energy through aerobic metabolism) due to the cardiovascular and neuromuscular changes that take place (a detailed discussion of maximal oxygen consumption is presented in Section 2).

Mitochondrial number and the levels of the proteins of oxidative metabolism, expressed per gram of muscle, do not increase in the heart in response to an endurance training program. The total amount of mitochondria increases, but the increase is proportional to the degree of muscle hypertrophy.

STRUCTURAL CONSIDERATIONS

From the standpoint of distance running, the large bones of the lower extremities and their ligamentous connections are of major importance. Endurance running strengthens bones, ligaments, and tendons and makes them less prone to injury. There is no good evidence of any difference in the effects of long, slow running as opposed to high-intensity interval running on the bones of adults. Both types of work appear to cause stronger and heavier bones. High-intensity running has been reported to delay the attainment of full height in growing school children while stimulating the growth of bone girth.

RESPIRATORY SYSTEM

The respiratory system can be divided into two general parts: the part that deals with external respiration and the part related to internal respiration. External respiration involves the movement of oxygen (O_2) from the environment, in through the mouth or nose, into the lungs, across the thin layers of tissue separating the air in the lungs from the blood circulating through the lungs (in small blood vessels called pulmonary capillaries), and into the blood itself. External respiration also involves the movement of carbon dioxide (CO_2) from the blood in the pulmonary capillaries to the environment, in a reverse manner to that taken by the oxygen described above. Internal respiration deals with the transfer of respiratory gases (O_2 and CO_2) from the blood to the working tissues and back into the blood. Skeletal muscles, for example those that operate the hip, knee, and ankle joints, are working tissues of primary importance in running; trunk muscles (in the stomach and back), arm muscles, and ventilatory muscles are of lesser importance when it comes to determining the amount of oxygen required by different muscle groups. During hard running and when breathing becomes very heavy, the ventilatory muscles naturally demand a greater amount of oxygen.

There are several characteristics of external respiration that help us understand the act of breathing or pulmonary ventilation. The lungs fill when ventilatory muscles (mainly the diaphragm, but also muscles that elevate and expand the rib cage) contract and increase the area within the chest cavity. This action lowers the pressure in the lungs and air flows in from outside the body where the pressure is greater. When the ventilatory muscles are relaxed, the volume in the chest decreases, increasing pressure in the lungs. This causes a flow of air to the outside where, in this case, the air is at a relatively lower pressure.

During normal-, resting-, or easy-work conditions, inspiring air requires the contraction of some ventilatory muscles (almost exclusively the diaphragm at rest); expiration during these easy-work conditions is a completely passive process — only relaxation of the ventilatory muscles is necessary—no muscular contractions are required. However, during harder work, when deeper and faster breathing is desirable, both inhalation and exhalation become active processes and energy is required for breathing during the entire cycle.

Respiratory rate or frequency of ventilation (f) refers to the number of breaths taken per minute; at rest, the number of breaths taken per minute averages about 10, but may vary considerably among individuals. The volume of air taken in and exhaled with each breath is referred to as tidal volume (V_T). The average tidal volume, or mean tidal volume ($\bar{V}_T$) at rest is about 500 cubic centimeters or one-half liter. The product of $\bar{V}_T \times f = \dot{V}_E$ (expired minute volume) and is expressed in liters of air breathed per minute. In the examples thus far referred to, $0.5 \times 10 = 5.0$ liters per minute, which is about average for minute volume of air breathed. If a person were to breathe in as deeply as possible and then measure the amount of air that could be forceably exhaled, the volume measured would be that individual's vital capacity (VC); it could be considered the greatest tidal volume possible. VC varies a great deal with body size, sex, and age and it could range from about 3 liters in a small person to over 6 liters in a larger individual. VC gives a rough idea of total lung volume; however, it is not a true measure of total lung volume, since a relatively large portion of air cannot be exhaled from the lungs (residual volume is the air that remains in the lungs, even after a forced maximal expiration and makes up about one-fifth of the total lung volume). Vital capacity is not normally altered as a result of training unless the training takes place during years of growth. Maximum voluntary ventilation (MVV) is the maximum amount of air that can be moved in and out of the lungs in one minute. The measurement is usually made for 12 seconds and converted to a minute volume. MVV is a combination of frequency and depth of ventilation and gives some idea as to the ability to ventilate the lungs.

In ventilating the lungs, or during *pulmonary ventilation,* consideration must be given to the amount of "useful" air being moved. With each breath, only part of the air reaches the lungs; the remainder of air is in the mouth, nose, and airways leading to the lungs. Since only the air in the alveoli (small, thin air sacs) of the lungs is available for exchanging gases with pulmonary blood vessels, the remainder of air in each breath can be considered as *dead space*. For practical purposes, the dead space volume remains the same during rest and work, which means that the deeper the breaths (or greater the V_T), the smaller percentage of $\dot{V}_E$ that is dead space. Conversely, fast, shallow breathing results in a greater percentage of dead space and less useful air volume per minute; the energy demands of fast breathing may also be greater.

During running, or any form of physical exercise or work that involves continuous use of large muscle groups, various nervous and chemical factors stimulate an increase in ventilation to meet the demand for an increased oxygen supply to the blood and for faster removal of carbon dioxide from the blood. Initially, there is an increase in both tidal volume and frequency of ventilation; however, tidal volume reaches a peak value before rate, and in fact it may decrease during very heavy exercise if frequency reaches very high values such as 80 or 90 breaths per minute.

The significance of the values of f and $\bar{V}_T$ reached during running is quite important. Consideration must also be given to ventilatory rhythm during running, although it is not as crucial as in swimming, where a breath can only be taken in rhythm with the turnover of the arms (except in backstroke, of course). Still most runners breathe in rhythm with their leg cadence. This ratio of breaths to steps taken most often falls into one of two patterns during hard running. Most common is a two–two breathing rhythm, where two steps are taken during inhalation and two during exhalation. At an average of 180 steps a minute, the runner breathing two–two would take 45 breaths a minute. The typical distance runner will take about 45 breaths a minute with a $\bar{V}_T$ of about 3.0 liters; this equals a ventilatory volume of 135 liters per minute. A smaller person would probably have a smaller tidal volume, and a larger person would have a tidal volume possibly as great as 4.0 liters. Generally, tidal volume during running at a fairly hard work load will peak out at about two-thirds of the individual's VC. For example, a small female with a 3.0 liter vital capacity would reach about a 2.0 liter $\bar{V}_T$; a larger female or average-sized man may have a 5.1 liter VC and would move about 3.4 liters per breath during comfortably hard running.

The significance of the depth and rate of breathing is in the degree to which the lungs become ventilated. For example, suppose that two runners (a woman and a man) each has a 4.5 liter vital capacity and, at a certain running speed, runner A breathes 3.0 liters per breath 60 times a minute (3.0 × 60 = 180 liters), and runner B has a 2.0 liter $\bar{V}_T$ and takes 90 breaths a minute (2.0 × 90 = 180 liters). Both are moving 180 liters of air in and out of their lungs per minute, but B is not as effective in ventilating all areas of his lungs, since his 2.0 liters of fresh air per breath makes up a smaller percentage of the total air in his lungs than does the 3.0 liters of fresh air ventilated by A for each breath. Also the energy expended may be greater for B. In other words, B's more shallow breathing is preventing him from ventilating his lungs as thoroughly as A can with a deeper ventilation, even though both are moving similar, total amounts of air per minute. The concentration of carbon dioxide will be higher, and that of oxygen will be lower in parts of B's lungs, compared with runner A, and continued performance at this shallow, "panting" ventilatory rate will become quite uncomfortable and less effective in terms of respiratory gas exchange and energy expenditure.

What are the limits that should be expected relative to frequency and depth of pulmonary ventilation? As mentioned earlier, tidal volume will usually reach a maximum of about two-thirds VC; this tidal volume will coincide with a frequency of about 45 to 50 breaths a minute. Since most distance runners take about 180 steps a minute, the next faster, logical frequency would be 60 breaths a minute – a two one or one two breathing rhythm (either two steps during inhalation and one step during exhalation, or one step breathing in and two steps breathing out). A two-one or one-two rhythm is quite common among middle-distance runners, especially during the latter part of a race; it is probably faster than necessary for long distance runs or for only moderately hard training runs. Tidal volume can remain fairly high during two-one breathing but any faster frequency becomes rather limiting. A one-one frequency (90 or more breaths a minute) becomes too shallow and is not comfortable nor effective for most people.

Similarly, an effort to breathe slower and with a very deep or large tidal volume is not effective, especially during hard work. In this case, in an effort to more completely inhale and exhale, the energy demands of the ventilatory muscles themselves become greater. Also the rhythm of slow, deep breathing is not as comfortable while running.

Basically, the depth and rate of breathing is not a matter for conscious thought; in most cases nature dictates the optimal pattern. However, if the runner is aware of a breathing difficulty, some attention to the act of ventilation may be well worth the time spent on it. A relaxed, rhythmical, "stomach" type of breathing should be the most effective.

A word should be said here about breathing through the mouth. The most effective way of ventilating the lungs is by breathing through the mouth; actually, through both the mouth and nose at the same time. The jaw should remain as relaxed as possible, and the face should remain expressionless throughout the respiratory cycle. Breathing only through the nose does not provide adequate amounts of air movement when working hard, and trying to continue nose breathing as the ventilatory demands increase becomes very difficult—eventually impossible for almost anyone.

The idea that it is dangerous to breathe hard in cold or freezing weather is greatly over emphasized. The body's ability to change the temperature of the air that it breathes in is so efficient that air entering the mouth at below-zero temperatures is heated to body temperature by the time it reaches the lungs. Cold, dry air sometimes causes an irritation and drying of the air passageways leading from the mouth and nose to the lungs, and this irritation from dryness is often blamed on the cold air. The cold itself should not be a matter for ventilatory concern. More will be said about running in the cold in a special section dealing with environmental considerations.

The portion of the respiratory system considered as dealing with internal respiratory activity will be covered in more detail in a subsequent section on aerobic metabolism. Here we are concerned with the transfer of oxygen from the blood into the muscle cells where, with the help of oxidative enzymes (chemical catalysts — protein in nature — that aid the chemical reactions of metabolism), stored fuel is aerobically burned. The amount of oxygen that can be used by the muscles is a critical factor in distance running, and it is greatly dependent on the type of muscle fibers present and their mitochondrial content (the location of the oxidative enzymes and aerobic power generation). The efficiency of this overall system is of great importance.

Naturally, the type and amount of training that a runner performs, as well as the genetic capabilities that are passed on from the parents, greatly affect this aspect of respiration. Many authorities consider this level of aerobic involvement to be the limiting factor in work capacity.

SECTION 2
Metabolism

Section 1 discussed specific adaptations of the important organ systems to an endurance running program. Now we want to enlarge upon specific aspects of metabolism involving these systems and, in particular, to discuss aerobic (oxidative) and anaerobic (nonoxidative) metabolism as they relate to distance running.

ANAEROBIC METABOLISM

It is impossible to completely isolate anaerobic metabolism from aerobic metabolism when discussing human performance, because we cannot function without an adequate oxygen supply. It is important to realize that both types of metabolism occur together. Changing our activity level or our external environment alters the relative importance of these systems, but never results in exclusively aerobic or anaerobic metabolism. As mentioned earlier, the anaerobic pathway is quantitatively less important in distance running, since the majority of the energy demand is met by aerobic means. However, the anaerobic system is qualitatively important because it is a quick source of energy during heavy work when the aerobic system cannot meet the entire energy demand, for example, at the beginning of a race or during a finishing kick at the end of a race. It is also important to look at the interactions of these systems during prolonged, submaximal work before and after training.

A good way to compare the interactions of these two systems is to look at the physiological differences in an individual before and after training and to discuss what these changes mean to distance running performance. When an individual exercises at the same submaximal work load before and after an 8 to 12 week running program, he or she will derive a greater percent of his or her total energy from the oxidative metabolism of fats and a lower percent from the oxidation of carbohydrates (blood glucose and muscle glycogen). Thus there is a sparing of carbohydrates or a slower rate in the depletion of both muscle and liver glycogen (the breakdown of liver glycogen provides the glucose needed to maintain blood sugar levels during work). This is important, for although fat is the main supplier of energy during submaximal work, hard continuous running (marathon running) cannot be maintained once muscle glycogen is depleted. Why a high metabolic rate cannot be maintained on fat alone is not yet clear, but there are a number of possibilities. More energy can be obtained from a gram of fat than from a gram of carbohydrate, but more oxygen is required to produce an equal amount of energy when fat is the substrate. The physiological consequences of this is that one requires more oxygen to perform a work load with fat as the only substrate than when fat and carbohydrates are metabolized. Therefore, when muscle glycogen is depleted and the muscles are metabolizing mainly fat, an individual will either have to increase oxygen consumption or decrease running speed. Competitive marathoners may already be running at a pace that demands over 80 percent of their maximal oxidative capacity. Since a further increase in oxygen demand could not be tolerated long, their only choice is to reduce the rate of running. Another possibility is that glycogen supplies metabolic substances that are needed to maintain the function of the oxidative pathway. In this case, a small amount of glycogen metabolism might be necessary to allow high rates of fat oxidation. Whatever the mechanism, there is a clear physiological advantage to reducing the rate of glycogen depletion from both muscle and liver by increasing the muscles' respiratory capacity, that is, the ability of muscle to consume oxygen, which increases as a result of the increase in muscle mitochondria (see Section 1). It has been reported that one cause of fatigue in marathon running is the depletion of muscle glycogen. Therefore, if one can retard the rate at which glycogen is utilized, one should be able to maintain a hard pace for a longer period of time. Figure 1 shows that when the muscle respiratory capacity (of rats) is increased with training (to different degrees by different lengths of daily running), less glycogen is depleted from liver and muscle during a 30-minute run (the ordinate shows glycogen remaining after the run in (1A) the gastrocnemius, a major calf muscle, (1B) the liver, and (1C) the total estimated glycogen left in both liver and all active muscles).

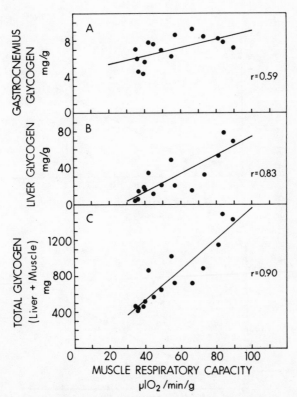

FIGURE 1. Correlation between the muscle-respiratory capacity of rats and (A) gastrocnemius glycogen, (B) liver glycogen, and (C) total glycogen remaining in active muscles and liver (muscle glycogen remaining was estimated from knowing the weight of the active muscle mass plus the glycogen depleted from a representative muscle).

Endurance training increases the concentration of the proteins involved in muscle respiration. Consequently, the trained muscle has a higher capacity for the oxidative metabolism of substrate (fat and carbohydrate) and hence a greater capacity for energy production. Figure 2A and 2B illustrate that muscle cytochrome c (a protein involved in muscle respiration) and muscle respiratory capacity are both significantly correlated with an animal's endurance, as reflected by run time to exhaustion. One may conclude from Figures 1 and 2 that the increased oxidative capacity of the working muscles allows for an increased fat metabolism, which reduces the rate and extent

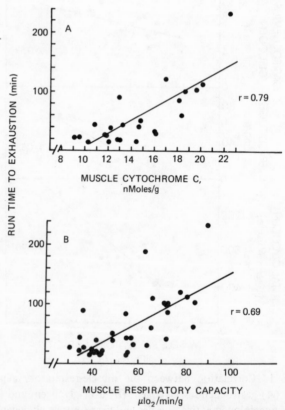

FIGURE 2. Correlation between run time to exhaustion and (A) Muscle Cytochrome C and (B) muscle-respiratory capacity in rats.

of glycogen depletion, allowing the more highly trained animals to run for a longer period of time. Table 4 shows that the more highly trained animals do indeed run longer.

TABLE 4. Effect of different training durations on exhaustive run among rats

GROUP	RUN TIME TO EXHAUSTION, MINUTES
10-Minute daily running	22
30-Minute daily running	41
60-Minute daily running	50
120-Minute daily running	111

One might ask how the increased muscle-oxidative capacity and corresponding increased capability for fat metabolism fits into a discussion of anaerobic metabolism. The answer is that a high-fat metabolism inhibits muscle glycolysis (the pathway of anaerobic metabolism) which, in turn, reduces the amount of muscle glycogen broken down to the anaerobic end product, lactic acid. (Remember, carbohydrate, in the form of muscle glycogen and blood glucose, is the only substrate that can be metabolized anaerobically). Figure 3 shows this phenomenon. When a standard submaximal bout of exercise is performed before and after training, the individual has lower muscle lactic-acid levels after training. The figure also shows that the highest glycolytic rate (level of anaerobic metabolism) occurs in the first few minutes of the exercise. This is because the heart is not pumping out enough oxygenated blood to the working muscles at the onset of work. It takes a minute or two for the circulation and muscle respiratory rate to reach a high enough level to meet the demands of the work through aerobic metabolism. Consequently, the anaerobic system works hardest in the first few minutes of work.

The higher muscle-respiratory capacity and fat-oxidative capacity do not alone explain the lower anaerobic-metabolic rate after training. During rest, mitochondria (the structure within muscle where oxygen is consumed) are relatively inactive. When work begins, muscles contract and break down the high-energy compound, adenosine triphosphate (ATP). The resulting products of ATP breakdown activate both the anaerobic and aerobic pathways. An individual's oxygen consumption during submaximal work changes very little

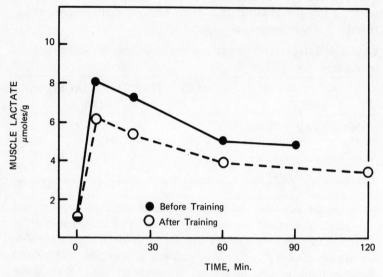

FIGURE 3. Muscle lactic-acid levels in a human subject performing the same submaximal work load before (● — ●) and after training (0 - - - 0).

as a result of a training program. However, following training, the exercised muscles contain more mitochondria; thus each mitochondrion needs to be activated to a reduced degree, compared to the mitochondria within untrained muscle, to reach the required oxygen consumption. Because each mitochondrion needs to be activated less, the muscles of trained individuals reach the steady level of oxygen consumption required for a submaximal work load quicker; hence the need for an anaerobic source of energy at the onset of work is reduced.

In summary, the increased mitochondrial concentration in the muscles of trained individuals allows them to utilize more fat and less carbohydrate. They also reach the required oxygen consumption for the work load faster, and hence the rate of anaerobic metabolism is reduced in the initial stages of work. These mechanisms combine to reduce the rate at which muscle and liver glycogen are utilized and therefore delay the onset of fatigue associated with glycogen depletion.

AEROBIC METABOLISM

In all physical exercise, the immediate source of energy is the splitting of adenosine triphosphate (ATP). The amount of ATP available in skeletal muscle is very small and is capable of providing energy for only a few seconds. However, creatine phosphate (CP) is also stored in the muscles and is readily available for the resynthesis of ATP. The CP stores are also quite limited and, in fact, the amount of energy available from ATP and CP concentrations in the muscles would provide for only about 15 to 20 seconds of heavy exercise. Furthermore, resynthesis of ATP must be provided for by either the anaerobic breakdown of glycogen (glycolysis) or the aerobic burning of fat or glycogen. In the former, the production of lactic acid is an ultimate waste product that must also be removed or that, in great enough concentrations, will bring about termination of the exercise.

In aerobic metabolism, a metabolic substrate (fat or carbohydrate) is "utilized" in the presence of oxygen and at the expense of a certain degree of oxygen consumption. The waste products of aerobic metabolism are water (H_2O) and carbon dioxide (CO_2), both of which are readily disposed of by the body.

When the intensity of running is low enough (below the level that requires a maximum rate of oxygen consumption – $\dot{V}O_2$ maximum) and after the first couple of minutes of exercise, the body is capable of adequately resynthesizing ATP aerobically and a buildup (or continued buildup) of lactic acid will not occur. This, for example, is the case in a comfortable eight-mile training run when the runner is at a submaximal "steady state" of work.

At the start of exercise (no matter how easy) or when a steady pace is interrupted by a burst of speed or an uphill stretch, the aerobic mechanisms cannot react quickly enough to provide the energy required and the extra energy is provided anaerobically. Figure 4 shows the portion of energy (expressed in milliliters O_2) provided aerobically and anaerobically during a bout of work involving changes in running speed (intensity of work).

Each energy demand must be met immediately and, since it takes a couple of minutes for the aerobic mechanisms to adjust to the demand, an anaerobic component comes into play with each new level of intensity (each increase in demand). When the energy demand lessens, the oxygen consumption returns to that required of the new

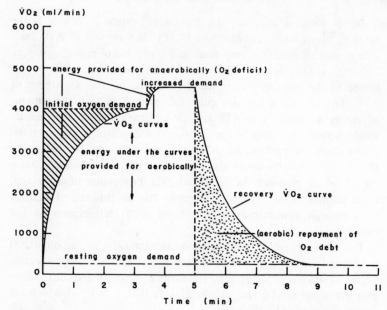

FIGURE 4. A descriptive picture of how aerobic and anaerobic mechanisms contribute to the energy demands of different workloads and recovery from exercise.

reduced work load. The oxygen consumed *above* the level required of the new reduced demand is referred to as oxygen "repayment" and can be thought of as repaying the oxygen deficit incurred during the earlier increases in work load when anaerobic processes were causing the development of an "oxygen deficit".

Depending on the intensity of work, the amount of O_2 repayment will vary in relation to the deficit — the repayment may vary from an amount that is equal to, to considerably greater than the calculated deficit, mainly as a result of the oxygen demands of the repayment process itself.

In any description of aerobic metabolism and its relationship to distance running, one question of considerable importance must be considered: What limits the amount of oxygen that can be consumed? Since it is well known that better distance runners have higher $\dot{V}O_2$

maximum values than less successful runners, it is only logical to investigate the possibilities.

Simply stated, four processes or physiological attributes play major roles in the body's consumption of oxygen: (1) The presentation of *an adequate supply of oxygen to the blood* that is flowing through the lungs. Further breakdown of this process would give individual consideration to pulmonary ventilation (the ability to move adequate amounts of air in and out of the lungs and ventilate all areas of the lungs), diffusion of the oxygen across the tissues of the lungs and pulmonary capillaries into the blood, and adequate perfusion of all parts of the lungs with pulmonary capillaries. (2) *The oxygen carrying capacity of the blood,* or the ability of the blood to take on adequate amounts of oxygen. Since most of the oxygen transported by the blood is carried in the red blood cells in combination with hemoglobin (an iron-containing protein substance), the amount of hemoglobin is the critical factor in potential O_2 carrying capacity of the blood. The pressure of oxygen in the blood, which is a direct function of the atmospheric pressure and concentration of oxygen in the atmosphere, also greatly influences the amount of oxygen that combines with the hemoglobin. However, under normal sea-level conditions, the O_2 pressure is sufficiently high to allow for nearly 100 percent saturation of the blood with oxygen. (3) *Oxygen transport* is often thought of as the most critical aspect of oxygen consumption. Basically, we are talking about cardiac output (the amount of blood that the heart can pump per minute — a function of the heart rate and stroke volume, or volume of blood pumped with each beat) and blood flow to the desired areas. A large cardiac output is of little consequence if blood is being diverted to an unneeded area. This is not usually the case; however, from the standpoint of oxygen consumption, blood that is diverted to the skin for the purpose of cooling might be thought of as detrimental. In a situation where cooling is of primary importance, the body becomes less interested in athletic performance and more concerned with maintenance of a desirable physiological environment. (4) *The ability of the working cells to utilize oxygen* is the final process to be considered in discussing the factors that limit oxygen consumption. Here the main variables are numbers of mitochondria (the sites of aerobic metabolism) and the presence of oxidative enzymes (chemical substances that provide for the conversion of fuel into energy, through the aerobic resynthesis of ATP). The type of muscle fibers in greatest concentration will also affect the ability of the muscle to utilize oxygen. Slow-twitch red fibers provide a greater potential for aerobic metabolism than do fast-twitch white fibers, which are more anaerobic-oriented muscle fibers.

We can now look at the possible limitations to reaching a greater $\dot{V}O_2$ maximum with a little more understanding of the processes involved. Under normal conditions, a healthy person is probably not limited by an inability to supply oxygen to the blood. Certainly, physical training increases pulmonary ventilation adequately. Runners who have trained at altitude, breathe more than necessary when they return to sea level. This indicates that the ability to ventilate more is there if needed. Research has also shown that healthy athletes are not limited by diffusion of O_2 from the lungs to the blood.

As suggested earlier, the O_2 carrying capacity of the blood is not limiting under normal sea-level conditions. However, at increasing altitudes (where the partial pressure of oxygen becomes decreasingly lower) or in a situation where the concentration of oxygen in the air is less than normal (an unusual situation and probably not encountered in an athletic event), then the percent saturation of oxygen in the blood can become low enough to seriously limit oxygen consumption. Naturally, if the individual has a low concentration of hemoglobin in the blood, then even 100 percent saturation of the available hemoglobin may not provide for as great an oxygen consumption as needed for reaching a better performance.

Considerable attention has been paid to limitations and relative importance of central and peripheral factors as they relate to $\dot{V}O_2$ maximum. If central oxygen transport, (cardiac output or the ability to pump out a lot of blood and carry a lot of oxygen) is the most critical factor, then there is a lot to be said for general cardiovascular conditioning for numerous sports. Developing a strong cardiovascular system through running would be good for swimmers, and the like.

If, on the other hand, peripheral factors (perfusion of the muscles and O_2 utilization by the muscles) are most crucial, then developing a 40 liter cardiac output may not be worth the effort if peripheral limitations can be met by a 35 liter cardiac output. This is probably of little concern to the average runner, since running training generally improves both central and peripheral components.

It is not always easy to say what limits what. For example, maximum heart rate and, subsequently, probably maximum cardiac output, are lower at altitudes than at sea level. Regardless of why cardiac output may be less at altitude, we know that the body is capable of a greater cardiac output (it demonstrates that ability at sea level). This would certainly suggest that cardiac output might be more limiting at altitude than at sea level, if indeed it limits under either condition. We must remember that the heart muscle itself requires a constant supply of oxygen and its own built-in defense mechanisms prevent it from working beyond the capacity of the coronary system (the network of blood vessels that supply the heart muscle with blood) to supply oxygen.

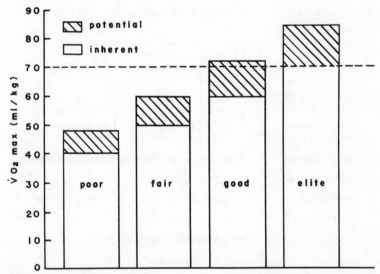

FIGURE 5. Changes in maximum oxygen consumption that might be expected with training, for runners with different, inherent starting abilities (the dashed line represents a level above which the potential for international participation might be possible). (Reproduced with permission from *Track and Field Quarterly Review,* **74** (3): 149, 1974, Ann Arbor, Mich. 48104, U.S. Track Coaches Assoc., Publishers.)

In the final analysis, it is becoming more apparent that we must look to the local muscle cells for the key to the limits of oxygen consumption. Certainly, it is quite accepted that genetic differences exist in the ability to utilize oxygen. $\dot{V}O_2$ maximum can be improved with training (apparently about 20%), and since it is quite acceptable that not everyone is born with the same $\dot{V}O_2$ maximum, it is easy to see that training will only elevate each individual's $\dot{V}O_2$ maximum, or potential $\dot{V}O_2$ maximum, a relative amount (see Figure 5). Some well-conditioned runners will beat less-conditioned, yet better-endowed runners. Unfortunately, the reverse will often be true.

As indicated earlier, the ratio of slow-twitch red to fast-twitch white muscle fibers may play a major role in determining $\dot{V}O_2$ maximum. Slow-twitch red fibers are known to have greater potential for oxidative activity and, even though aerobic training does increase the oxidative capacity of all fibers, the runner with greater predominance of oxidative, red fibers will have a certain genetic advantage in endurance activities. (Figure 6 summarizes factors that affect aerobic capacity.)

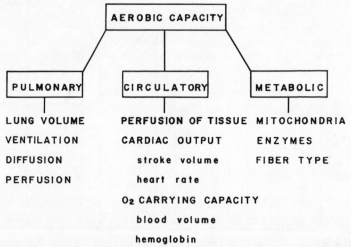

FIGURE 6.   Factors that influence aerobic capacity ($\dot{V}O_2$ maximum).

RELATIVE IMPORTANCE OF AEROBIC AND ANAEROBIC METABOLISM

When a runner starts a distance race, the energy demands are met by both aerobic and anaerobic processes. During the first couple of minutes of the run, the oxygen consumption (the oxygen used in aerobic metabolism) steadily increases until the amount of oxygen that is used reaches the amount needed for performing the work.

If the intensity of work (more specifically, the effort put into running or *speed* in flat races) demands more energy than can be provided for aerobically, some energy will be produced anaerobically.

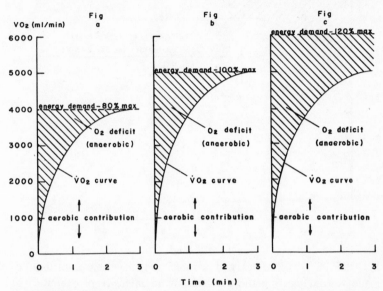

FIGURE 7. $\dot{V}O_2$ curves and aerobic and anaerobic contributions made toward meeting the energy demands of various intensities of exercise (*7A:* submaximal work, *7B:* maximal work, *7C:* work that demands more energy than can be delivered through aerobic mechanisms alone).

Figures *7a, 7b,* and *7c* show the aerobic and anaerobic contributions of various running intensities for a runner who has a $\dot{V}O_2$ maximum of 5000 milliliters per minute. In each case, the $\dot{V}O_2$ curve levels off after about two or three minutes of running. The initial slope of this curve is greatly dependent on the intensity of work, that is, the faster the running pace, the steeper the curve. Figures *7a, 7b,* and *7c* also show the differences in the anaerobic component of the total energy expended at different running speeds. In Figure *7a,* the O_2 deficit (the part of the energy provided for anaerobically during the time the oxygen consumption is not meeting the requirements through aerobic metabolic pathways) is about 3000 milliliters during the first three minutes of work. During this same three minutes,

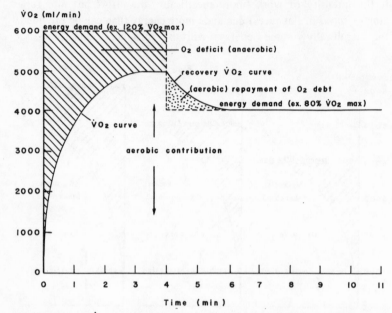

FIGURE 8. $\dot{V}O_2$ curves and aerobic and anaerobic contributions made toward meeting the demands of an intensity of exercise that is beyond the capabilities of $\dot{V}O_2$ maximum, followed by an adjustment to submaximal work.

about 9000 milliliters of oxygen are consumed. If the runner continued at the same pace for 10 minutes, the remaining seven minutes of work would result in the consumption of 28,000 milliliters O_2 (seven minutes × 4000 milliliters per minute).

In Figure 7*b*, even through the $\dot{V}O_2$ curve is steeper, the O_2 deficit incurred during the first three minutes of running would be a little greater than that in 7*a*, – about 3500 milliliters. Should the running continue at a speed requiring 100 percent of $\dot{V}O_2$ maximum for 10 minutes, the remaining 35,000 milliliters O_2 (seven minutes × 5000 milliliters per minute) would theoretically be provided for aerobically without further anaerobic involvement. However, it is not possible

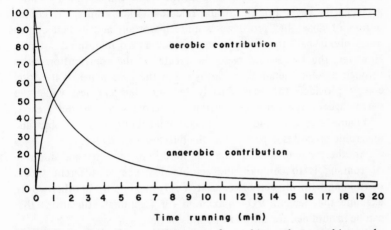

FIGURE 9. Relative contributions of aerobic and anaerobic mechanisms depending on the duration of a race.

to completely separate or shut on or off either aerobic or anaerobic processes and, particularly at work loads that require at or near 100 percent $\dot{V}O_2$ maximum, there will continue to be substantial energy contributions made anaerobically resulting in limited work due to continued production and accumulation of lactic acid. At running speeds that require 100 percent $\dot{V}O_2$ maximum, the duration of work will be about 10 minutes (see below).

In Figure 7c, the running intensity is beyond the intensity that can be met solely through aerobic mechanisms. Again, with the increased intensity, the $\dot{V}O_2$ curve is a little steeper, but the requirement is great enough that the anaerobic component during the first two minutes is about 5000 millimeters, which is probably representative of the runner's maximum oxygen debt.

If the degree of anaerobic involvement is maximum for this particular athlete, then further running (beyond about two minutes) at this intensity would not be possible. The only choices the runner has are (1) to stop or (2) to slow down to a speed for which all energy required could be provided aerobically (see Figure 8).

From the above discussion we realize that the intensity of running greatly determines how long an individual can continue without a change in pace. For short- and middle-distance events, the contribution of anaerobic processes is quite important and in fact contributes about half the energy required for a two minute all-out run. However, the longer the race, the greater is the contribution made through aerobic metabolic pathways, and the percentage of the total energy provided for anaerobically becomes less and less while the percentage of the aerobic contribution becomes greater and greater.

Figure 9 shows the approximate contributions of aerobic and anaerobic processes depending on the duration of the race.

Another way to look at the relationship of intensity and duration of running is to compare the aerobic demands of different speeds of running with the aerobic capacity ($\dot{V}O_2$ maximum). In other words, examine the percent $\dot{V}O_2$ maximum (or fractional utilization) that can be maintained for different periods of time.

Each individual will consume a certain amount of oxygen while running steadily at any submaximal speed ("submaximal" refers to a speed that requires a $\dot{V}O_2$ less than $\dot{V}O_2$ maximum). A curve can be constructed by connecting the $\dot{V}O_2$ measured at several running speeds, and the $\dot{V}O_2$ required of other speeds can be estimated from this speed/$\dot{V}O_2$ relationship (Figure 10 shows a typical $\dot{V}O_2$/speed relationship constructed from four measured speeds and oxygen consumptions). By then calculating the $\dot{V}O_2$ that represents the runner's best time for various distances and comparing this $\dot{V}O_2$ to the individuals $\dot{V}O_2$ maximum a curve relating percent maximum to time run can be constructed. Figure 11 depicts this relationship. It is important to realize that the critical variables are percent maximum and *duration,* not distance. For example, a runner who can run two miles in 9 minutes will be working at about 100 percent $\dot{V}O_2$ maximum, but a runner who can run only 20 minutes for 2 miles will not be able to work at 100 percent $\dot{V}O_2$ maximum for the full two miles. However, the latter runner may well manage 100 percent $\dot{V}O_2$ maximum for 9 minutes as does the better runner, but will not cover two miles in that time.

Figure 11 is constructed from data representing a variety of well-trained runners, and consideration must be given to the fact that different levels of physical condition, the type of training being performed, and possibly the relative amounts of different muscle fiber types will shift the curve slightly up or down at one or both ends.

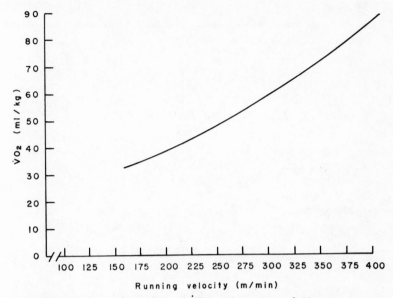

FIGURE 10. The relationship of $\dot{V}O_2$ and running velocity.

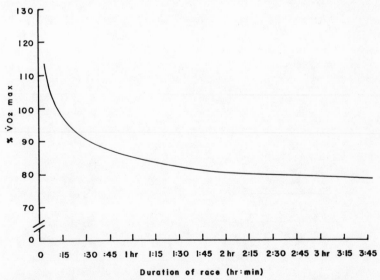

FIGURE 11. The relationship of the duration of a race and the relative energy demands of running, expressed in percent $\dot{V}O_2$ maximum.

SECTION 3
Environmental Considerations

TEMPERATURE

The human body is far better equipped to handle cold temperatures than it is hot. This is particularly true when we are concerned with hard physical work or distance running in various environmental conditions. Since a great deal of the energy produced by the body is released in the form of heat, the temperature-regulating mechanisms are doubly stressed during exercise in conditions of excessive environmental heat. On the other hand, since physical exercise does internally heat the body, running in the cold presents little handicap until temperatures are low enough to cause possible damage to exposed body parts.

As the body temperature increases, whether as a result of internally or externally imposed heating, physiological adjustments take place to combat excessive heat buildup. Although some heat is released from the body by the lungs and the process of ventilation (this is readily seen among dogs when they pant to eliminate heat through the lungs and mouth but is of limited value among humans), the human body best combats heat buildup through perspiration. The sweat glands put out fluid as well as electrolytes, which when it evaporates from the surface of the body, lowers the skin temperature. Blood flow is diverted to the periphery (the blood vessels close to the skin), and the blood is cooled as it passes through the cooled areas.

The environmental conditions greatly determine the effectiveness of the sweating process: (1) the humidity and temperature of the ambient air and (2) the flow of air around the body. If the atmosphere is highly saturated with water vapor, as on a day of high relative humidity, then evaporation of sweat from the skin is not very complete and, without evaporation, cooling cannot take place. This is why on days of high humidity, it appears that sweating is more profuse (mainly since the sweat does not evaporate well); consequently, the surface of the skin and the clothing become extremely wet.

Working hard in a situation where there is little flow of air around the body produces the same result; with inadequate air flow, a layer of warm, moist air builds up around the body and a very warm, humid miniatmosphere exists in which the individual must work. This is easily noticed when one runs with the wind, where wind velocity and running speed produce a very still-air situation. This is also often true when running on a treadmill if care is not taken to circulate the warm, moist air away from the exercising runner.

On dry days, especially during running where air flow is good, sweat evaporation is very rapid and cooling is quite effective. However, it sometimes appears that little sweating is taking place (due to rapid evaporation, which leaves the clothing and skin relatively dry), and it may become quite misleading as to how much body water and electrolytes are being lost. To compound the problem, the sensation of thirst usually lags behind the body's need for fluid replacement, and it is not uncommon for a distance runner to unknowingly develop quite a fluid and electrolyte deficiency.

As has been alluded to, loss of body fluids and electrolytes (which are lost along with sweat) are detrimental to continued performance at an optimal rate. Continued sweating without adequate fluid replacement places extra demands on the circulatory system and exposes the runner to serious adverse affects of overheating, including heat stroke and heat exhaustion.

Since body temperature tends to rise directly with loss of body weight through sweating, it is important to attempt continuous fluid replacement during the period of running. It is also desirable to replace sodium and potassium losses by ingesting fluids that provide these electrolyte solutions. The American College of Sports Medicine recommends that the concentration of sodium should be less than 10 milliequivalents and the concentration of potassium should be 5 milliequivalents, per liter of water; sugar concentration should not excede 2 and ½ percent (2.5 grams per 100 milliliters of water). Commercially available products should be diluted to meet these recommended concentrations.

Drinking large amounts of fluids during the hours preceding a distance run is not entirely beneficial. If taken more than about 30 minutes before the run begins, fluid may cause discomfort as a result of having passed through the kidneys and into the bladder. It is therefore more desirable to injest fluids about 15 to 20 minutes before the run and about every 20 minutes during the run. Amounts should be about 200 milliliters at a time, during the run, and about double that amount before the race. It is also important to practice taking fluids during practice runs so the experience will not be a new one in a race situation.

Normally, races and long training runs that last less than about one hour can be undertaken without planning for fluid replacement. However, remember that prerace warmup and possible prerace heat stress can turn a relatively short distance race into a very stressful situation and should be adequately adjusted for.

The practice of sponging or wetting the body during a race has not been proven to be physiologically beneficial; it does not hold down body temperature effectively as can fluid injection. Still, it does produce a feeling of relief to some runners and probably is not harmful unless used in place of fluid replacement.

In summary, body temperatures can reach very high levels (above 104° F) during endurance runs, and fluid loss can be as great as 8 to 10 percent of body weight. Beyond about 2 or 3 percent loss of body weight, the effects of further fluid loss become more critical, and care must be taken to replace both fluids and electrolytes at regular time intervals to prevent reduction in performance. Hydration (fluid intake) before a long run can be beneficial, but only to a limited degree. This procedure is best undertaken during the last 15 to 20 minutes before the race begins. Among the disadvantages and dangers of excessive fluid loss are reduced circulation to exercising muscles (which reduces work capacity) and ultimate loss of ability to continue putting out sweat. Severe adverse effects of further temperature rise can result, including the possibility of death.

Acclimatization to heat does take place over a period of a week or two with the results that less perspiration is put out (fluid loss is more efficiently controlled), and the sweat contains less concentration of electrolytes. Wearing light, porous clothing can aid in reducing the effects of heat buildup as a result of direct exposure to the sun, while allowing for evaporation of sweat from the surface of the skin.

One final consideration should be given to running in hot climates and that is the time of day. If at all possible, long runs and especially races should be scheduled either during early morning hours (usually the coolest time of day in terms of ambient temperature) or after sunset, which often is the driest time of the day as well as being a time the extra heating effect of the sun cannot add to the already adverse problem of working hard in a warm temperature.

As has been mentioned earlier, the adverse effects of running in the cold are usually far less encountered than are those related to heat. Under all but the most extreme conditions, the body can produce enough heat during running to adequately maintain normal body temperature. Probably the main concern in the cold is for prevention of excessive exposure of bare skin to the low temperature. This is especially true of areas such as the ears and fingers where blood flow diminishes and chances of freezing can become a reality.

The main adjustment to be considered in regard to running in the cold is clothing. The amount of clothing that will provide adequate protection, yet will not cause an overheating problem, is the critical concern. Clothing should be used in layers. One heavy outer garment may be too much after a few minutes of running, but if discarded, protection is inadequate. The advantage of several thin layers of clothing is that, as the body heats up one or more layers can be removed without the danger of loss of protection.

The best material for cold weather protection is something that protects against the elements, yet allows flow of moist air from the body. The purpose of protection against the cold is defeated if it is of a type that traps moisture between the body and the outer clothing, subsequently causing perspiration to collect in the clothes, which presents a further hazard, especially upon cessation of exercise. Usually wool and cotton materials are best suited for cold weather; rubber-lined suits protect against wind and cold extremely well, but these do not allow evaporation to take place, and they are not desirable, except during early warmup and after exercise for heat retention.

It is not wise to wear metal bracelets, watch bands, and jewelry against bare skin if the metal parts are exposed to freezing temperatures; these metal items conduct heat rapidly and may lead to freezing of some surface tissue.

A wool cap that can be rolled up or pulled down over the ears is ideal head gear, and light wool mittens are suitable for the hands. It may be desirable to use a wool liner inside an outer shell mitten in extreme cold. In either instance, mittens are usually better than gloves, since the latter isolate the fingers from each other and inhibit most desirable warming of the hands.

Some types of socks that come up on the ankle are good for very cold weather, but the feet usually have less trouble than do other extremities in keeping warm.

The often-expressed concern about freezing the lungs in cold weather is not the serious problem that it is made to seem; the body's ability to heat inspired air is extremely efficient and, by the time that even below-freezing air reaches the lungs, it has been heated to body temperature. The irritation that is sometimes felt in the throat and lungs is usually due to dryness of the air, which dries out the normally moist lining of the air passageways. This can cause some discomfort but should not be taken for freezing of lung tissues. When it is realized that cross country skiers race and train regularly at very low temperatures, it should not be hard to accept the fact that running in the cold is not nearly the hazard that some would think.

If the skin is exposed to the atmosphere, actual freezing of tissue normally will not occur until the temperature is below 20° F; if the skin is exposed when it is moist, freezing may take place at temperatures just under 30° F. The best insurance is some protective clothing that can be easily carried.

As far as performance in cold, environmental conditions goes, if the temperature is not low enough to demand excess clothing, physiologically, performance should be enhanced. This is mainly because there is less need for available blood to be diverted to the skin for cooling. This function of the circulatory system still takes place — even sweating will commence in freezing conditions if work is heavy enough — but usually heat that is produced during exercise is welcome to some degree in cold weather. Also, heat elimination is better and performance is often better as a result.

ALTITUDE

Two general considerations should be given to altitude running. First, there is the problem of the effects of altitude on performance at altitude; second, we must consider the use of altitude training as a special way of preparing for races at sea level.

Any discussion of altitude racing should examine the acute effects of altitude (how can a runner expect to be affected in a race upon acute exposure to altitude?) and acclimatization to altitude (what adjustments can be expected with a period of training at altitude and how might training be changed to be most effective?).

The effects of altitude on distance running have been extensively studied — at least as they relate to the sea-level athlete. Among the systems of the body that are affected by altitude, the oxygen-transport system is the one that causes the most concern for the distance runner. Events that require major emphasis on strength, speed, or neuromuscular coordination do not appear to be adversely affected at altitude.

Running events that are shorter than 800 meters are not adversely affected by altitude; in fact, the sprints are probably aided slightly by the reduced air density at altitude. The 800 meter event is about the turning point — reduced air resistance is balanced out by reduced aerobic capacity. Beyond 800 meters, there is a definite adverse effect of altitude on performance. Not only does this effect vary with the distance being run but also with the altitude at which the race is run. More accurately, the *duration* of a race, not the *distance* run, is the more crucial factor. Figure 12 gives a method for figuring the degree to which a runner might expect to be affected in different races at different altitudes. Remember that the values shown in Figure 12 are for a sea-level athlete who has had considerable training time at altitude; a newcomer could expect even greater losses in performance.

Before continuing, it should be clarified that this discussion on altitude running will basically be limited to quite a narrow range of altitudes, specifically the 4000- to 10,000-foot (1200 to 3000 meter) range. This "moderate" altitude range encompasses most situations where altitude training or competing is likely to occur.

The amount, or, more specifically, the concentration of hemoglobin (the oxygen-binding substance in the red blood cells) greatly

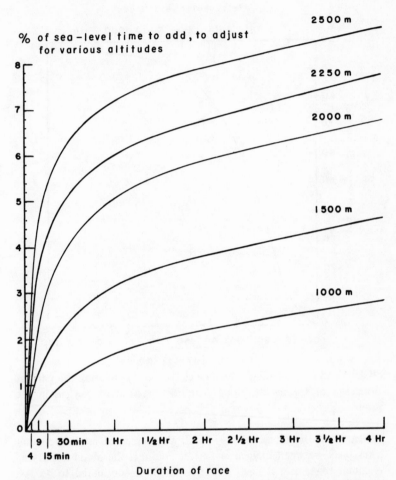

FIGURE 12. Differences in percent sea-level performance that can be expected to be added to sea-level best times for various race distances at different altitudes. (From *Track and Field Quarterly Review,* 75 (4): 39, 1975, Ann Arbor, Mich. 48104, U.S. Track Coaches Assoc., Publisher.)

determines how much oxygen can be carried from the lungs to the working muscles, since most of the oxygen is transported in combination with hemoglobin. The pressure under which the oxygen is

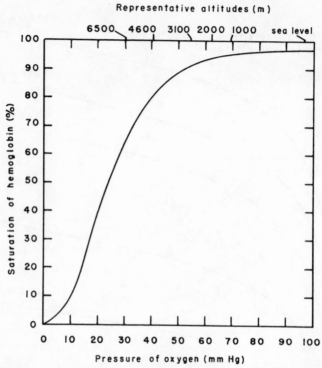

FIGURE 13. Oxyhemoglobin dissociation curve, relating the percent saturation of O_2 in the blood with the pressure of oxygen in the blood.

presented to the blood greatly affects the degree of association that takes place between oxygen and hemoglobin. If the blood is carrying as much oxygen as it has a capacity for, it is considered to be 100 percent saturated with oxygen. In a normal human, the blood becomes nearly 100 percent saturated with oxygen each time it passes through the lungs—provided, of course, that the pressure of oxygen as it is presented to the blood is sufficiently high. Figure 13 shows the configuration of the oxyhemoglobin-dissociation curve, which relates the pressure of oxygen with the percent saturation of oxygen in the blood. It is interesting to note that an increase in PO_2 (pressure of oxygen) above that experienced under normal sea-level conditions does little or nothing toward increasing the percent saturation.

On the other hand, as the PO_2 drops, as it does with increasing altitude, there reaches a point where the blood is not as saturated with oxygen as it is at sea level, and an equal amount of blood does not carry as much oxygen at altitude as it does at sea level. The relationship of PO_2 (which is directly related to the degree of altitude) and oxygen saturation is not a linear one, and therefore the effect of running at 5000 feet (1524 meters) altitude is not half of what might be expected at 10,000 feet (3048 meters). Also, by referring to Figure 12, it is seen that little or no effect should be noticed up to an altitude of about 3000 feet (914 meters); however, there is a considerable difference between 5000 feet and 8000 feet (2438 meters), which is also a 3000 foot difference in elevation.

The human body makes rapid adjustments to minor altitude changes and, at rest or during light work, a healthy person will notice no effect of the altitude. It is an easy matter for the oxygen-transport system to deliver usual amounts of oxygen by increasing blood flow and ventilation slightly, thus compensating for a slight drop in oxygen concentration in the blood.

Working hard, as is the case in a distance race, is a different situation. First, a distance runner is already working at maximum intensity (at least, as intensely as possible for the distance involved), and the compensatory mechanisms, which provide for a maintenance of adequate oxygen delivery during rest and light work, are not readily available. If the athlete could increase ventilation and cardiac output, he or she would already have done so at sea level with a resulting performance improvement.

Possibly, factors that do not limit sea-level performance may become more limiting at altitude. Ventilation and oxygen transport are probably capable of meeting most demands of the working muscles at sea level; this may not be the case at altitude. More specifically, the ability of the working muscles to utilize oxygen may be more limiting at sea level than during performance at altitude. The problem appears to be more of a peripheral one, rather than an inadequacy in central circulation and respiration. However, at altitude, there is reason to believe that the ability of the central, cardiorespiratory system to supply oxygen to the working tissues may play a more obvious role in limiting performance. This would provide support for the observations that highly trained, sea-level athletes would not benefit as much as less-conditioned athletes, from a period of altitude training. The better-trained athlete has already made adjustments to the training stimulus; any additional adjustment comes from the new stimulus of altitude while untrained athletes have both training and altitude as new stimuli. It does appear that altitude training brings out the best in a runner who has good potential but is not performing up to capabilities.

The initial loss in $\dot{V}O_2$ maximum when exposed to moderate altitude, is 10 to 20 percent depending on the altitude. The improvement in $\dot{V}O_2$ maximum at altitude, following six to eight weeks of altitude training, is about half of the amount lost. In other words, at 7500 feet (2286 meters), acute exposure results in about a 15 percent drop in $\dot{V}O_2$ maximum; after several weeks of acclimatization, the maximum oxygen consumption is about 8 percent below the original sea-level value. Interestingly, the loss in performance time is only about 8 to 10 percent upon acute exposure, and it improves to within 3 to 6 percent with altitude training. In effect, performance loss is not as great as is loss in $\dot{V}O_2$ maximum, which suggests that either the lowered air density (and, consequently, lowered air resistance) results in a slightly lower oxygen demand for any given running speed, or anaerobic capacity is not lowered as is aerobic capacity, with the result that total energy available is relatively greater than would be calculated from aerobic sources alone. The latter explanation would not be feasible for very long races, but a lowered energy demand of running does appear to be a likely factor at all distances.

Novice altitude competitors must waste little time in performing their specialty for time, thus learning as soon as possible just where they stand and how their race is affected. At moderate altitude, there appears to be no need for several days of easy work before harder training or racing can take place.

In early altitude races, particular care must be given to race pace; an even pace is more vital to success than is true of sea-level races. Interval training sessions do not always paint a realistic picture of the effects of altitude, and it is easy to develop a false sense of security regarding the intensity that can be maintained for a prolonged hard effort.

When a few weeks of training at altitude have been completed, the runner will usually find that a race effort feels about the same as at sea level, but it is a little slower (Figure 12 can be used to estimate a reasonable pace). However, the final kick is just as fast as normal, probably because the combined aerobic and anaerobic energy sources are not as far off sea-level values as are the aerobic factors alone, and the factor of muscle speed is probably unaffected at altitude with proper training.

Several studies indicate that the best results are reached in altitude races when the runners alternate their training between altitude and sea-level sites. This is also encouraging, since one need not fear that a few days at sea level will destroy any previously developed altitude acclimatization. On the contrary, a few days (possibly as many as 12 days or more) back at sea level seem to help altitude performance. A possible explanation why remaining steadily at altitude may not produce the same effect as does alternate exposure to altitude and sea level is that since less oxygen can be presented to working muscles at altitude, the muscle fibers are not as stressed in their ability to utilize oxygen and lose some of their ability to process large amounts of oxygen. The exact mechanisms involved certainly need further study.

Regarding the type of training most effective for altitude races, in addition to including some prolonged hard runs or intense, long intervals, we must examine maintenance of usual speed during shorter interval runs. Recovery time should be lengthened, if necessary, to allow for normal training pace. This is particularly important if subsequent races are anticipated back at sea level.

Normal training mileage can probably be continued as can normal workouts, in most respects. Again the recovery periods should be sacrificed first, then length of hard runs, and lastly intensity. Some training sessions should be geared to subjective feelings of stress, others to predetermined training pace. In addition to alternate reexposures to sea level, it can also prove useful to take runs or hikes to higher altitudes for several hours at a time.

One advantage of trips to altitude is that altitude training seems to bring out the potential of a runner; acceleration of reaching the potential goes hand in hand with this concept. Another possible advantage of altitude is that often the intensity of steady runs is lessened somewhat and, even though the oxygen-transport system is working hard, mechanical stress may be at a lower level, and injuries may be fewer and less severe.

Altitude training has undoubtedly made the difference in the running careers of some athletes; others have not shown any changes in performance. As in any system of training, there are individual responses, and what benefits (or harms) one runner's performance may show no effect (or an opposite effect) on another runner's performance. Possibly, just getting into a different environment is worth the change for some athletes.

SECTION 4
Nutrition

Discussion of the nutrition of running is difficult, for although the science of nutrition has been actively investigated for hundreds of years, much is still unknown. The basic foods have been classified according to their protein, carbohydrate, and fat content. The essential amino acids (amino acids are the basic components from which proteins are made, and essential amino acids are those that cannot be synthesized by the body and hence must be included in the diet) have been identified. A number of vitamins and minerals have been recognized as essential to good health. However, much is still to be learned about the ideal combination of the proteins available (both vegetable and animal) as well as the optimal percentage of protein, carbohydrate, and fat in the daily diet. The function and minimal daily requirements of many of the vitamins and minerals are yet unknown. These unknowns make nutritional recommendations difficult, and the large increase in caloric expenditure associated with distance running further complicates the evaluation of good nutrition. Do the requirements for the essential amino acids, minerals, and vitamins increase in parallel with the increased caloric needs, or do the needs for some of these essential substances increase out of proportion to the caloric increase? This question has not been satisfactorily answered, and it will not be answered until the functional roles of the essential foods are clearly understood. One cannot adequately study whether the dietary requirements of a particular vitamin or mineral increases with physical activity until one knows the function of the substance. This area of research into the nutritional needs of the physically active adult men and women and growing children remains essentially unexplored and a major challenge to the scientist who is interested in physical activity. Because of this lack of knowledge, it is impossible to make specific recommendations based on scientific facts. We can only discuss the strengths and weaknesses of the dietary practices in general use, with an evaluation of their practical value to the distance runner. The discussion will be concerned with both the chronic (daily) dietary needs and specific dietary alterations preceding and following a big race (acute dietary needs).

CHRONIC DIETARY NEEDS

The main source of energy during work is derived from the metabolism of fats and carbohydrates. Daily running increases the caloric requirement, and one must increase the intake of fat and carbohydrate or lose body weight through the metabolism of stored fat. If you are overweight, when you begin running, you may be able to go several months without increasing your caloric intake. The extra caloric expenditure will be met by the stored fat. However, as your fat stores diminish you must increase your caloric intake, because carbohydrate stores (in liver and muscle) are quickly depleted, and it is undesirable to utilize body protein. Body protein will be used as an energy source when fat and carbohydrate stores are gone. This will result in muscle wasting and a reduced physical performance.

It can be concluded that one must increase caloric intake to match caloric expenditure in order to maintain a constant body weight. It is recommended that the diet contain 10 to 15 percent protein, or 35 to 40 grams per day (most Americans probably exceed this recommendation). It is not clear whether a runner should maintain, increase, or decrease the percentage of protein in the diet when increasing caloric intake. With training, a runner decreases body fat and increases body protein. The heart hypertrophy and the increase in the level of the skeletal muscle proteins responsible for oxidative metabolism all require an increased protein availability. Therefore, one can speculate that the protein content of the diet should be maintained at 10 to 15 percent of the dietary intake. The total amount of protein consumed would increase as a result of the increased caloric intake required to meet the extra caloric expenditure of running. The increase in dietary protein should adequately supply the amino acids needed for the increased synthesis of new body proteins in the response to training. However, if you continue to lose weight despite an increased caloric intake, you may be in a negative-protein balance (metabolizing more protein than your diet supplies); this could be corrected by increased supply of dietary protein. At the opposite extreme, it is possible that your diet contains too much protein. The extra protein would be converted by the liver to carbohydrate and, if your caloric intake exceeds your expenditure, the carbohydrate will be used to synthesize fat. This would result in an increased body weight that would signal you to decrease your caloric intake.

A diet that is high in protein (greater than 50 percent of the caloric requirement), but normal in caloric requirement can be dangerous. The liver has a maximal metabolic rate and it cannot effectively convert large amounts of protein to glucose for oxidation. Excesses in a particular amino acid can impair the absorption of a related amino acid that has a common transport system.

The type of protein is as important as the total amount. All of the essential amino acids must be present, or a negative-protein balance will result. The diet should be centered around grains, fresh vegetables, fruits, and berries with some skim milk and eggs included to insure an adequate supply of all of the essential amino acids, minerals, and vitamins. Meat is not necessary, but a strict vegetarian diet (without milk or eggs) could lead to a protein imbalance unless the vegetables, fruits, and grains are combined judiciously. Fish and lean meat can be used to supplement this vegetarian diet.

Fat and carbohydrate are the main sources of energy during work. Fat is ideal from the standpoint of storage efficiency as it supplies 9 kilocalories of energy per gram while a gram of carbohydrate yields only 4 kilocalories. Fat is stored in droplets while carbohydrates are stored with water. This hydration further reduces the energy equivalent of carbohydrates. Although a gram of fat contains potentially more energy, the generation of this energy through oxidative metabolism requires more oxygen. Therefore, the consumption of 1 liter of oxygen metabolizing pure carbohydrate yields 5 kilocalories compared to 4.7 kilocalories when fat is metabolized. Expressing this in terms of the high-energy phosphate bonds (ATP) that provide the energy for muscle contraction, 6.2 and 5.6 molecules of ATP are produced per molecule of oxygen when metabolizing carbohydrates and fats respectively. This makes the metabolism of carbohydrate 9 percent more efficient than fat, and hence carbohydrates are the preferred substrate at heavy work loads where the efficiency of energy production is important. For example, a work load that requires 3 liters of oxygen per minute, with carbohydrate as a substrate, would require 3.3 liters of oxygen when utilizing fat. Distance runners generally metabolize both carbohydrate and fat, except at the end of extremely hard, long runs where muscle glycogen may become depleted. Adequate carbohydrate and fat intake can be obtained from a diet containing grains, vegetables, fruit, milk, and eggs supplemented occasionally with fish and lean meat.

It is usually difficult to develop a vitamin deficiency because vitamins are common in our normal diet. However, if you are on a restricted food intake, overcook your foods, or eat only certain types of food, deficiencies can occur. You can develop a deficiency in the fat soluble vitamins (A,D,K) if you have trouble absorbing dietary lipids. Whether runners need vitamin supplements, and, if so, which ones and in what amounts, has not been adequately investigated. Intuition suggests that supplements are not needed, because the presence of the vitamins in the normal foods contained in a well-balanced diet allows any increased need to be met by the increased food intake of the active person. If you are fasting or on a restricted food intake, vitamin supplements can protect you from vitamin deficiency. An excess of vitamins in the diet can lead to malabsorption problems and toxicity in some cases (especially the fat soluble vitamins). Therefore, one should be careful not to take an oversupplement of any vitamin.

Vitamin D is not really a vitamin (it is more correctly a hormone); for it is synthesized in the body upon exposure to sunlight, and hence it is not an essential dietary substance. Runners who are outdoors a few hours each day with little clothing need not worry about vitamin D deficiency. Vitamin D in excess is toxic and has been correlated with heart disease.

Vitamin A occurs commonly in vegetables, fish, eggs, and liver and is stored in the liver in large quantities. For these reasons, it is difficult to develop a deficiency in vitamin A. Deficiency signs would be loss of appetite, fatigue, muscle pain, loss of hair, and scaly skin. Vitamin A in excess is also toxic.

Deficiency of vitamin K is rare for it is synthesized by intestinal microorganisms and occurs in green vegetables. This vitamin is not stored, and a deficiency could result if your diet lacks green vegetable and you are taking an antibiotic that inhibits your intestinal microorganisms.

The B vitamins are widely distributed in foods, and many are synthesized by the intestinal microorganisms, hence deficiencies are rare. Vitamin B-1 (thiamine), important in metabolism, occurs in many foods but little is synthesized by intestinal microorganisms. Deficiency is rare but can occur when the diet is restricted to highly refined foods or by prolonged cooking of foods. Vitamin B-2 (riboflavin), important in oxidative metabolism, occurs in most foods and is synthesized by intestinal flora, hence deficiency is rare. Vitamin B-6 (pyridoxine) functions in metabolism and deficiencies are rare. Biotin functions in metabolism and is widely distributed in foods. Deficiency can result from eating raw eggs, since a protein in egg whites binds tightly to biotin. Pantothenate is widely distributed in foods and synthesized by intestinal flora; a deficiency in this vitamin cannot even be produced experimentally. Nicotinamide nucleotides function in metabolism and exist in high concentration in cells, but have short life spans from a standpoint of biological activity (high turnover). Tetrahydrofolate functions in metabolism, is widely distributed in foods, and is synthesized in the intestine. Deficiency can be produced with inadequate diet, poor absorption, or overcooking of food. Vitamin B-12 (cobamide) deficiencies can result from a strict vegetarian diet. However, deficiencies take many years to develop, and symptoms may not be apparent for 10 to 15 years.

A deficiency in vitamin C (ascorbic acid) leads to defective bone and blood vessel walls (vitamin C deficiency produces general problems in collagen formation). When vitamin C is oxidized, it quickly loses its biological activity. Temperature accelerates this process, and thus much vitamin C activity is lost through cooking. Processed foods lose their vitamin C activity when exposed to air for extended periods (e.g., orange juice stored in a refrigerator). Fruits, vegetables, liver, and kidneys are good sources of vitamin C.

The function of vitamin E is unknown. It is widely distributed in many foods. A deficiency can produce degeneration of skeletal muscle, and a high polyunsaturated fatty acid diet can aggrevate vitamin E deficiencies.

Minerals like vitamins are important dietary substances. They are needed for normal cell structure, and cell physiology and metabolism (e.g., calcium and phosphate are structural components of bone, while sodium, potassium, calcium, and magnesium play important roles in muscle physiology). Whether runners need extra supplements of one or more minerals is unknown. As with vitamins, the mineral needs of the physically active have not been adequately studied. Sodium (Na+), potassium (K+), chloride (Cl−) are needed in large amounts but occur in quantity in our diets, hence deficiencies of these minerals are rare. There have been some studies on the chronic (not considering the acute changes during or directly after exercise) blood-serum levels of these ions following a prolonged program of distance running. The general finding is that there is no change in Na+ and Cl− ions but a slight tendency for K+ ion to decrease. However, the decreases reported are generally small and not significantly different from control values. Furthermore, blood-serum levels may not reflect total body ion concentration. One study reported low, total body K+ levels (measured using a radioactive K+ ion) with no change in blood-serum levels. In this study, however, the subjects were untrained previous to the study period, and the environmental temperature was extremely hot (range 80 to 105°F). No change in total body K+ was observed in a similar group of subjects training in a cool environment.

Dietary recommendations concerning Na+, Cl−, and K+ ions based on the available research data are difficult to make. Supplements of Na+ and Cl− are probably not necessary, and excess dietary Na+ could aggrevate the tendency for runners to develop low concentrations of body potassium by increasing urinary excretion of K+. The tendency toward low body K+ can certainly be prevented by eating natural foods that are high in K+ such as fruit juices (especially grapefruit and tomato), dried blackeyed peas, soybeans, cabbage, carrots, and nuts (instant coffee is also a good source for those who drink coffee); artificial supplements are not necessary.

The need for magnesium (Mg++) is less than that for Na+, K+ or Cl−, but its dietary availability is also lower. Studies have shown the blood serum levels of this ion to decrease following prolonged running, but there is no evidence about chronic changes in total body concentration with distance running. Many of the foods that are high in K+ are also high in Mg++, particularly nuts, dried soybeans, and blackeyed peas. A diet containing Mg++ rich foods should prevent any deficiency in this ion.

Calcium (Ca++) deficiencies do occur but can be avoided by eating foods high in Ca++ such as milk, cheese (particularly swiss), and fish. Phosphate deficiencies are rare, and foods high in Ca++ are generally high in phosphate.

Iron (Fe++) deficiency is perhaps the most common of all mineral deficiencies, especially in women. The general symptom of iron deficiency is fatigue. It can be diagnosed by a blood test and prevented by eating foods high in iron. The best source of iron is liver and kidney, foods that are not particularly popular in our culture. Wheat germ, wheat bran, hulled sunflower seeds, and rice bran are also good sources of iron.

Any conclusions drawn concerning optimal nutrition for distance runners are at best guesses due to the lack of scientific knowledge. However, it seems safe to suggest that all of the essential amino acids (protein), fats, carbohydrates, vitamins, and minerals can be obtained from a judiciously chosen natural-food diet consisting of grains, fresh vegetables, fruits, berries, milk and eggs, supplemented by fish and lean meat, if so desired. These foods will meet your dietary requirements provided that they are not overcooked or left standing for prolonged periods. The natural-food diet will be cheaper than refined foods and artificial supplements, and it will reduce the possibility of the toxic effects associated with certain vitamin overdoses. Finally, natural foods provide superior supplements to the synthetics, since one never knows how long vitamin and mineral pills have been exposed or what percentage of their biological activity has been lost.

A few words about fasting as a method to improve running is needed because of its increased usage. Under proper supervision, one- to three-day fasts may be beneficial if, for no other reason, than aiding one to maintain as little body fat as possible. While fasting, the percentage of energy derived from fat and protein metabolism increases. In this process, the concentration of the specialized proteins that aid in the metabolism of fats may be built up. Thus periodic fasts may be beneficial if they increase the muscle's fat-metabolizing capacity, which would reduce the rate of glycogen depletion during a run. Fasts allow the intestinal tract to clean out or become void of digestive waste. This may be beneficial to the digestive system. The only thing that we know to be true is that fasting will result in a loss in body weight. If you have excess fat, this loss may benefit you provided that the excess protein metabolism does not produce muscle weakness. The other possible beneficial effects have not been demonstrated through scientific experimentation and hence remain speculation. There are certain situations where fasting should be avoided. If you are already extremely light, further fasting may result in excessive body protein breakdown and muscle wasting. This is undesirable, since it will reduce the force-generating capacity of your muscles. Fasting should not be used for two or three days before a race. During a fast, muscle and liver glycogen depletion will occur early in a race if you run hard. You will be able to run for extended periods, at a low to moderate pace (where fat metabolism can handle the entire energy demand), but you will not be able to maintain a hard pace (one that requires glycogen metabolism). For the same reason, one should not train hard while fasting. Hard running while fasting will produce muscle and liver glycogen depletion and result in hypoglycemia. It could also result in ketosis, a condition associated with high rates of fat metabolism and increases in blood acidity.

What weight should you run at? Your ideal running weight depends on your skeletal size, but generally most runners find that they run best when they are 10 to 20 percent below the recommended weight for their height. For example, if you are 5 feet 11½ inches, your running weight might ideally be as low as 140 to 145 pounds. It is better to be lean than fat. Excess fat serves no useful purpose. It reduces your endurance by increasing the energy cost of any distance run. Pick the weight you want to run at, and adjust your daily, caloric intake to reach this weight. Always weigh yourself at the same time each day (usually in the morning, before running or eating is best) and on the same scale if possible.

ACUTE DIETARY NEEDS

In the late 1930s, scientists reported that subjects eating a high carbohydrate but normal caloric diet outperformed subjects on a normal, mixed diet. Thirty years later, this concept was studied in more detail by measuring muscle glycogen before and after exhaustive exercise. The subjects worked on a bicycle ergometer at a work load requiring 75 percent of their maximal aerobic capacity. They were able to exercise three times longer when the test followed a three-day high-carbohydrate diet than when it followed a protein and fat diet (it should be emphasized that the total caloric intake was 2800 kilocalories in both diets). The investigators found a good correlation between work time and initial muscle-glycogen content (the mean preexercise muscle-glycogen levels were 0.63 grams per/100 grams of muscle and 3.31 grams per/100 grams of muscle, respectively for the protein and fat, and carbohydrate diets).

Subsequent to these studies, it was found that muscle-glycogen levels could be raised even further if the high-carbohydrate diet was preceded by a long run that depleted muscle-glycogen stores before supercompensating the muscle glycogen on the high-carbohydrate diet. With this technique, muscle-glycogen levels as high as 4 grams per/100 grams of muscle can be obtained.

A final modification of these dietary manipulations requires that a depletion run be made one week before an important race (one and one-half- to two-hour run at a moderate-to-hard pace). This run is followed by a protein-fat diet (carbohydrates are kept as low as possible) for three days, and then, for three days before the race, one eats a high-carbohydrate diet. With this procedure, muscle-glycogen levels have approached 5 grams per/100 grams of muscle (normal muscle level might be 1.5 grams per/100 grams of muscle). This dietary procedure has become known as the glycogen-supercompensation technique. This practice has become widely used, but because it is poorly understood by many runners, its misuse has presented problems. Most runners have no problems with the first day of the procedure. Since they are fit, they complete the depletion run with no problem. During the next three days on the low carbohydrate diet, a normal caloric intake should be maintained by eating proteins and fats. A higher than normal caloric intake is undesirable because excess protein will be converted to carbohydrate, which may cause muscle-glycogen levels to rise prematurely. In fact, it may be best to keep the caloric intake slightly below normal during this phase of the diet. It is impossible to run long or hard during this period; not only is muscle glycogen low, but also blood glucose and liver glycogen are below normal levels. If you attempt to run hard, you run the risk of developing hypoglycemia (low blood sugar). The brain depends mainly on blood sugar as its source of energy; with hypoglycemia, dizziness and blackouts can occur. Thus long hard runs should be avoided during the low-carbohydrate phase of the diet. During the last three days, the diet should be high in carbohydrate, but the total, caloric intake should be normal.

Some have interpreted a high-carbohydrate diet to mean an increase in caloric intake that is above normal. This interpretation is a misconception, the term high here means an increased amount of carbohydrates, not calories — the total caloric intake should be normal or, at most, 200 to 300 calories above normal. For example, if you normally consume 2800 kilocalories, the first three days after the depletion run, you might eat 1500 kilocalories of protein and 1300 kilocalories of fat. The next three days, during the high-carbohydrate phase, you consume 2300 kilocalories carbohydrate and 500 kilocalories protein and fat.

The final muscle-glycogen level reached is not linearly related to the carbohydrate intake. After muscle-glycogen levels reach 3 to 3.5 times the normal resting levels, increase in muscle glycogen stops, regardless of how much carbohydrate is consumed. It does no good to markedly increase caloric intake (i.e., eating five loaves of bread). An excessive food intake can lead to severe indigestion, abnormally high blood-triglyceride levels (triglyceride is a type of fat), and excessive weight gain. On the carbohydrate phase of the diet, you should only do light running because hard or long running will use muscle glycogen and result in lower levels on the race day. There is evidence that this procedure, which increases muscle glycogen concentration 3 to 3.5 times, can improve performance in races that are in excess of six miles. This dietary procedure should not be used in races shorter than six miles because glycogen depletion is not likely to occur in runs of 30 minutes or less.

Glycogen supercompensation results in a 1 to 2 kilogram weight gain because each gram of glycogen is stored with 2.7 grams of water. In long races, this extra weight is not a handicap, since water loss through sweating can exceed 3 to 4 liters. The water released during glycogen metabolism helps prevent the dehydration that can result from excess sweating during long races on hot days.

One must use the above described dietary procedure with caution. Be especially careful not to run hard or long on the low-carbohydrate phase of the diet or to overeat during the high-carbohydrate phase. Because the glycogen supercompensation procedure requires six easy days of running, it is recommended only preceding marathon races, and then only once or twice a year. For other marathons and for all races of shorter duration, a modified procedure in which the depletion run is performed four days before the race may be more suitable. For example, if the race is on Saturday, the depletion run is performed on the preceding Tuesday. No carbohydrates should be eaten the rest of Tuesday. A high-carbohydrate diet should then be eaten from Wednesday through Friday. With this technique, muscle-glycogen levels reach concentrations that are 2.5 to 3 times normal resting levels (with the low-carbohydrate phase included, muscle-glycogen levels reach 3 to 3.5 times normal levels). This modified procedure reduces the number of easy days from six to three. We do not know yet how fast detraining (the process whereby the body organs lose the advantages gained through training) occurs. Six days may be long enough for the trained muscles to lose some of the increased oxidative capacity they had gained through training. Certainly, if repeated often, a detraining could result. It is possible that the advantage of the seven- over the three-day procedure (slightly higher muscle-glycogen levels) are offset by a slight reduction in the muscle-oxidative capacity following six days of rest. There have been no controlled studies on the relative effectiveness of these two procedures. For marathon distances and above, it is recommended that you try both to see which one works best for you. For races shorter than a marathon, the modified technique should be used, because muscle-glycogen levels will be high enough to prevent muscle-glycogen depletion. This technique eliminates the possibility of developing hypoglycemia, a condition that can develop during the low-carbohydrate phase of the seven-day procedure, and it limits any possibility of detraining as a result of a six-day rest.

Some concern has been expressed over the possibility of developing high blood-triglycerides while on the high-carbohydrate diet. Trained runners often have low blood-triglyceride levels. The triglyceride levels will rise while on the high-carbohydrate diet, but these transient increases will probably not exceed the normal range. The exact extent of the rise and whether or not the transient rise affects the resting blood-triglyceride levels once a normal diet is resumed is unknown. Without data, one can only speculate on this issue. Our speculation is that the chronic levels would not be affected by periodic, transient rises. However, if your blood lipids are abnormally high, you should probably avoid any glycogen-supercompensation, dietary technique.

SECTION 5
Training and Running Technique

TYPES OF TRAINING

Over the years, training techniques have evolved mainly by trial and error. Because people have been running for so long, a good many techniques used today can be justified not only by the results they have produced but also scientifically. The main value of a scientific evaluation of running technique is to help develop new techniques and to utilize the optimal combination of presently available techniques. Finally, science can help lay to rest the myths that have developed about certain training techniques, especially those that have been advanced as a panacea for all.

It might be said at the outset, before going into specific types of training, that the main ingredient to successful running is a consistent, year-round training program. Training is not like money; it cannot be put in a bank and saved. We need to continually work our body systems in order to continue to develop them. Some of the muscle adaptations discussed earlier occur relatively quickly, within 8 to 12 weeks of training. This occurs because the proteins involved have fairly short life spans. We can increase their levels rapidly, but their levels can decrease just as rapidly once we stop training. We cannot, of course, stress ourselves hard everyday, since this leads to chronic fatigue and to the deterioration of the beneficial, adaptive responses to training. We know from animal experiments that there is a minimal amount of running required to produce any effect, and that there is a maximal training level above which no further training benefits occur. Our training program should be balanced so that one or more hard training days are followed by an easy day of running. One cannot give a formula that applies to all, but you can use certain signs to determine your optimal sequence. Some have found success by alternate hard and easy days while others train two or even three hard days in succession before taking an easy day. The sequence that you use depends on your personal life style and the type of training you do. If your training contains hard-interval workouts, the alternate hard/easy sequence may work best for you, while a runner depending more on long, moderate runs may find the two-hard/one-easy sequence to work best. Whatever sequence you develop, it must remain flexible. You should never run hard on a day when you feel fatigued. Fatigue is a sign that your body is not ready to be stressed. You must run easy until you feel rested and ready to run hard again. The purpose of the easy day of running is to allow your body to recover from the previous hard training while still allowing you to maintain at least a minimal training stimulus. Three to five miles of moderate running is enough on an easy day. This type of work will allow you to recover from your hard training while maintaining a minimal training stimulus. Just as your weekly schedule must contain a sequence of hard and easy days, so must your yearly program. It is desirable to take three to five easy weeks after a tough, long race or competitive season (i.e., three or four times a year). You should not stop running entirely, since a good deal of detraining occurs within five weeks. Instead, you should maintain a light program of three to five miles of daily running. Whatever distance you choose, it should be enough to maintain a minimal training stimulus while allowing you to recover from a hard race or season of running.

Every day of running should start with five to seven minutes of easy running, a similar period of flexibility exercise, and then a few more minutes of easy running. The warmup and flexibility exercises are important parts of each training session. The warmup allows the heart to increase its rate per minute and volume per beat so that adequate amounts of oxygenated blood reach the working muscles. It allows muscle and body temperature to rise slightly, which provide for an optimal metabolic and physiological environment. The warm-up also allows time for fat to be released from its storage sites into the blood so that the working muscles can utilize it. (In this way, the warmup itself helps reduce muscle-glycogen depletion by giving the muscle an adequate supply of fat.) A warmup should not exceed 10 to 15 minutes of easy running, and it should be begun as close to the actual start of the workout or race as possible. A more prolonged warmup could decrease muscle glycogen; all of the beneficial effects are gained within 10 minutes. Too long a time interval between the warmup and the workout or race is not desirable, since heart rate and muscle temperature rapidly return to resting levels. The flexibility exercises are important. The stress of running may cause shorter resting muscle-fiber lengths in the active muscle groups. The muscles then pull on their tendons and limit joint flexibility. This can lead to tendon inflamation. Most runners have experienced achilles tendonitis, which generally results from overtight calf muscles. Tendon inflamation in the knees is also common because of tightened thigh muscles. The joint limitation can eventually lead to sciatic nerve problems. All of these injuries can be prevented by daily flexibility exercises and leg massages whenever muscle tightness develops. More details on injuries, their cause, and suggested cures are presented in Section 6.

There is no one training program to fit all runners. Each of us needs to develop a program to fit our individual requirements and life style. With this understood, the following discussion covers a variety of types of running that could be part of any long distance runner's program. Specific workouts are mentioned as examples, and they are intended to illustrate general types of running so that you may understand each one and develop your own program.

In general, training can be designed to selectively condition various systems. The relative importance of each is an individual matter and depends on many factors, primarily the type of race on which the individual wishes to place the greatest emphasis.

As should be the case for any strenuous activity, a period of several weeks of easy running should precede any attempts at a vigorous training schedule of any kind. This early "pretraining" period might be thought of as injury-prevention training, since it can serve as a break-in period for the beginner or as a readjustment to hard work for the previously active runner. It is worthy to note that even easy running can be a considerable stimulant to the person who is in poor physical condition, and the term "easy running" might better be phrased as "comfortable" running. Once at a relatively good level of condition, training can be geared to meet the more specific needs of the individual.

ENDURANCE AND AEROBIC POWER TRAINING. The word endurance has various definitions and meanings depending on the event. Perhaps it is most suitable and useful to describe endurance for running in relative terms: the ability to work close to one's maximum aerobic capacity for a prolonged period of time. To increase one's endurance is dependent on increasing the ability to work at high, relative work loads for extended periods of time.

The type of training needed for endurance improvement is quantitatively very important for long distance runners (six milers and longer). It produces the adaptations in the cardiovascular, respiratory, and neuromuscular systems that were discussed in Sections 1 and 2. In particular, this type of running increases the aerobic (oxidative) capacity of the slow, red fibers and, to some extent, the fast, red fibers.

Both continuous and intermittent running can be included in endurance training. Continuous runs should be of moderate intensity, and the distance can be one that would take 20 minutes to an hour or more to negotiate. As the runner gets more fit, the speed of the run can be increased, but the relative effort will not be affected too much. This might be considered "comfortably hard" running.

Intermittent runs may be at a slightly faster pace (about two-mile race pace), and the recovery periods should be brief (shorter than the work period) and should involve jogging. For example, a five-minute miler might run repetitive 440-yard runs in 80 to 85 seconds each, with a 110-yard jog following each run. The best distances for intermittent runs are those that require up to about five minutes of running. Shorter runs (such as 440's) must, necessarily, be interrupted by short recovery periods; longer runs are followed by recoveries about equal to or shorter in time than the time taken for the preceding run itself.

Recent reports by Scandinavian researchers indicate that there is also considerable merit in shorter interval workouts, in the development of aerobic capacity. "Short" intervals are designated as consisting of repeated work bouts of 60 to 90 seconds with about one-third to one-half that time for recovery, and "short-short" intervals would be 10 to 20 seconds work followed by 5 to 15 seconds recovery, repeated

20 to 60 times (possibly broken down into two 30-repeat sessions with a few minutes between sessions). The important point in this intermittent, aerobic-type training is that the work intensity is *not* great (it is usually a speed that could be maintained steadily for about 10 minutes), but the recovery periods must be short so that the conditioning stimuli are constantly present, even during the recoveries.

In both the continuous and intermittent types of endurance running, the key element is constant movement. You are running throughout the workout, and thereby you are placing a prolonged stimulus on the heart and skeletal muscles. This type of training is important because it increases your aerobic (oxidative) work capacity and gives you the capability of running at a relatively high percentage of your maximal oxidative capacity for extended periods of time. As mentioned earlier, it is particularly important to those training for races over six miles, where you need not only a high-oxidative capacity but also the ability to maintain this high metabolism for extended periods of time.

The weaknesses of endurance running (both continuous and intermittent) are: (1) it may not adequately train the fast, white fiber type of skeletal muscle; (2) it tends to decrease the speed of muscle contraction by reducing the concentration of myosin ATPase in the fast, red fiber type (remember that myosin ATPase controls the rate at which ATP is broken down and hence the rate of muscle contraction); and (3) it reduces the anaerobic (nonoxidative) capacity of the fast, red fiber type in skeletal muscle. The consequences of these negative aspects depend on the length and type of race you are training for. The white fibers are not recruited in moderate running on flat terrain (this explains why endurance running fails to train this type of fiber). Therefore, if you are a marathon runner and you race only on flat courses, you probably would do well with only endurance running. However, white fibers are recruited in hill running. If you run on hilly courses, your thigh muscles (especially the upper, front outside area of the leg) that contain a relatively high number of white fibers, will fatigue. Two- to six-mile racers, in particular, need to consider the limitations of moderate endurance training. In this type of running, speed is important in order to get away from your opposition, and anaerobic metabolism is particularly important in the beginning and end of the race. Both speed and anaerobic metabolism are compensated when moderate endurance running is used exclusively.

PACE RUNNING. Pace running is a variation of the intermittent endurance training described above. It involves running sustained intervals at a pace slightly faster than your race pace and is designed to train both aerobic and anaerobic metabolic systems. The running interval should be two to five minutes in duration and, between efforts, you should rest completely. Your rest interval should be about as long as your run interval or, at least, until your heart rate has recovered to 100 beats per minute or less. For example, if you are training to run a 14-minute, three-mile run, your run interval might consist of a mile in 4 minutes and 35 seconds followed by complete rest, until your heart rate returns to 100 beats per minutes (three to four minutes). You might run three to five such intervals. The important ingredients of this type of training are (1) to maintain a hard effort for at least two minutes, and (2) to rest completely between intervals until your heart rate has recovered to 100 beats per minute.

The highest degree of anaerobic metabolism occurs in the initial stages of the interval. Initially, your heart is not pumping enough oxygenated blood to the working muscles so they derive a good deal of energy from the anaerobic pathway. When energy is produced anaerobically, muscle glycogen is broken down to the metabolic end product, lactic acid. The reason why the interval should last at least two minutes is to allow for maximum rates of anaerobic metabolism and, thereby, to produce high-muscle lactic acid levels. The interval should not exceed about five minutes in length, since longer intervals would require a slower pace resulting in more aerobic and less anaerobic metabolism.

Muscle lactic acid is a good indicator of the degree of anaerobic metabolism. In this type of workout, you want to obtain the highest possible muscle lactic-acid levels. High lactic-acid levels are desirable, since they indicate a training of the anaerobic system. In addition, the muscles are conditioned to tolerate a high concentration of lactate, a condition that frequently develops at the beginning and end of races. Figure 14 illustrates the importance of the length of the interval if the intensity is moderately hard. The figure shows an individual running a pace workout at five different lengths, from 10 seconds up to 3 minutes, with equal rest intervals. Peak-muscle lactic acid was not reached until the runs reached three minutes in length. Pace runs of less than 60 seconds clearly do not stimulate muscle glycolysis long enough to produce high-muscle lactates.

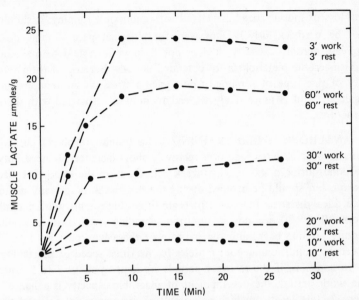

FIGURE 14. Muscle lactic-acid levels in a subject performing interval runs for five different lengths of time — 10 seconds work, 10 seconds rest up to three minute work, three minutes rest.

The other important aspect of pace running is that the rest intervals consist of complete rest and not continued slow running, even though light activity minimizes venous pooling of blood in the legs. Complete rest is necessary so that heart rate will recover toward resting levels during the rest interval. This more adequately insures that you can perform the next run at an adequately demanding pace. By running slowly during the rest period, you maintain a fairly high circulation to your muscles, and you keep the muscles' oxidative metabolism elevated. Both of these processes help to lower muscle lactic-acid levels during the rest period. Since one purpose is to build the highest possible lactic-acid levels, it is undesirable to run slowly during the rest period. On the other hand, if you are running two races in a meet, it would be desirable to run slowly for 5 to 10 minutes following the first race. This would increase the rate of muscle-lactic acid removal and thereby speed your recovery.

Pace running tends to counteract the major limitations of endurance running. It trains the anaerobic (nonoxidative) pathway and retards the loss of muscle speed associated with endurance running. It should not be used exclusively, however, for although pace running does increase aerobic capacity, it does not train your system to maintain a high-aerobic metabolism for extended periods. Because of the intensity of this type of running, it puts greater stress on the tendons and ligaments and is more likely to lead to injuries associated with these structures.

ANAEROBIC/SPEED TRAINING. This training involves repetitive runs at near all-out speed over relatively short distances. It need only be done during a six- to eight-week period before the important race season, but should be avoided during the final week before any major race. Ideal distances for such efforts are those that require work periods from 10 to 70 seconds in duration. Running much farther would require holding back; and the purpose of these workouts is to build speed by conditioning your muscles for maximal speed of shortening.

In addition, if the recovery periods are kept to about 3 to 5 times the work period, the development of anaerobic capacity is enhanced. Here, lactate levels are high as a result of the greater intensity of the runs (Figure 14 shows that the shorter workouts do not produce high lactates for the relatively lower intensity work required of pace running). An example of a short-distance, high-intensity workout would be 8 to 10 times 30 seconds hard with one and one-half minutes recovery after each run.

This type of training builds speed by yet unknown mechanisms. It may increase the rate of nerve activation of muscle or the speed of muscle shortening. Shortening speed would be enhanced by increasing the myosin ATPase activity (the special protein controlling the rate of muscle contraction).

HILL RUNNING. Training on hills is important, especially to the road racer who will have to race on hilly courses. To maintain the same race pace while running uphill requires increased force, and this in turn increases the energy demand. The increased force for the added work on hill running is supplied by the recruitment of the fast, white fibers. These fibers are not extensively used during moderate running on level terrain. Therefore, hill training is a prerequisite to successful hill racing. Without hill training, you will be requiring untrained fibers (fast, white fibers) to work every time you race a hill, which will result in muscle fatigue and an impaired performance.

Hill training is of value to track runners as well. It not only recruits the fast, white fibers but it also stimulates the anaerobic pathways within all muscle fiber types. Hill training places a severe strain on tendons, ligaments, and joints, and hence each hill workout should be limited to not more than 10 to 12 hills, two or three times a week. It is often not easy to find hills that are long or steep enough to adequately train all muscle fibers. An ideal hill is 100 to 300 yards long with a 5 to 10 degree slope. This type of hill will require 20 to 60 seconds of hard running (hills of 400 to 500 yards are good to run but extremely difficult to find). If you are lucky enough to live in a hilly region, it is best to map out a circular course with five or six hills (within a six mile area). Run each hill two times in succession, for a total of 10 to 12 hills within six or seven miles of running. For those living in flat regions, you may have to settle on one or two hills, repeating each one five or six times. Generally, it is good practice to run hard up and slightly over the top of a hill and ease up on the downhill side. Occasionally, you should run hard downhill, if you are training for road racing. This should be limited to a few hills per workout due to the joint trauma involved with hard downhill running.

To summarize: your training program should encompass the various elements described here — endurance and aerobic training, pace, hill running, and speed and anaerobic running. The emphasis that you place on each depends on your needs and the race that you are training for. Endurance and aerobic running build the capacity for aerobic metabolism and the ability to maintain a high-metabolic rate. Pace training increases anaerobic metabolism and retards the negative aspects of endurance training (i.e., decrease in speed and anaerobic metabolism). Hill running trains the fast, white fibers as well as giving a general stimulus to anaerobic metabolism. Speed/anaerobic training allows for maximal speeds of muscle shortening that may be called upon in a tight competitive race and stimulates an increased anaerobic capacity.

RUNNING TECHNIQUE

A book on distance running would not be complete without a discussion of proper form. People of different builds and heights will, of course, encounter varying problems when they are running, and technique may vary slightly when they are running on roads as opposed to tracks. Although running is a relatively simple skill, there are surprising differences in efficiencies of running between individuals. Perhaps the most important technique involves foot placement. Your feet lead your body and determine the direction in which the force of muscle contraction is applied. The foot should hit the running surface in line with the desired direction of movement. However, some runners direct their feet out so that the toes are pointing 45° off the desired course of travel (frequently called duck-footed action). Such placement directs part of the generated force to the sides instead of straight ahead in the desired direction of movement. It takes a conscious effort to correct improper foot placement. One good exercise is to run down a straight line painted on the running surface. Try to place each foot on the line as you run. Another common error among inexperienced runners is to land too high on the ball of the foot. The best landing position is on the outside center area (almost flat footed), and in fact many marathon runners hit on the outside portion of the heel and roll forward, driving off the ball of the foot. It is poor technique for distance runners to run on their toes for two basic reasons. One, your calf muscles absorb the major shock when running this way and will fatigue more rapidly than if the load of landing is distributed across the whole foot. Two, by running on your toes you lose force. Muscles contract more forcefully if they are stretched before they contract. Landing on your heel or flat footed stretches the calf muscles, which then contract more forcefully and drive your body forward.

Correct arm action generally develops naturally. You should remember not to carry your arms too high but let them hang in a natural position. Carrying your arms too high requires your arm and shoulder muscles to work unnecessarily, which wastes energy. It may also interfere with proper ventilation. The arms should be held at their natural position, bent 90° at the elbow, with palms held inward and slightly cupped (hands are in a natural position—this requires the least amount of energy for position maintenance). The arm should swing slightly forward when the opposite leg comes forward, to help maintain body balance and forward direction.

The body position depends on the running terrain. A slight, forward lean is desirable to help direct the forces of muscle contraction into the forward direction. Too erect a body position frequently leads to an upward bounce with each stride. This exaggerated upward bounce requires force that should be directed in the forward plane.

Optimal-stride length is dependent on your leg length. You want your stride to be long enough to allow your center of gravity to be slightly in front of your driving leg when pushing off the running surface. Too short a stride wastes energy by requiring you to take more steps and by not permitting you to take full advantage of the forward energy generated by the previous muscle contraction. Too long a stride allows your center of gravity to fall behind your drive leg and increases the force of your upward motion (upward bounce noticeable) while retarding the forces in the forward plane. In general, each individual unknowingly selects the optimal stride length, based on training and racing demands.

In hill running, it is necessary to shorten the stride slightly in order to maintain the center of gravity over the drive leg. It is sometimes necessary to exaggerate your forward lean in order to direct force up the hill and not out from the hill. In going downhill, your stride should lengthen to maintain your center of gravity slightly in front of your drive leg. Lengthening your stride on the downhill will help you maintain your balance while taking maximal advantage of the down slope in aiding your forward acceleration.

SECTION 6
Clinical Aspects of Distance Running

Athletes in general and distance runners in particular are people who get the most out of their genetic endowment through training. Training, although it takes on various forms and names, is designed to stress many systems of the body. It is based on a principle of increasing loads, often referred to as "overload," and a runner theoretically is subjected to a new load after recovery from each previous load.

The systems that are stressed by training of one type or another include the cardiovascular, respiratory, musculoskeletal, gastrointestinal, nervous, genitourinary, hematological, metabolic, and endocrine. When stresses are too great, the athlete breaks down; the overuse is too much for some inherent weaknesses in some particular system or systems.

The distance runner is one of medicine's most challenging patients. Physicians who are traditionally trained in disease are not accustomed to the problems of individuals seeking their maximum cardiopulmonary, neuro-muscular, and metabolic state. There are few practioners who are prepared at this time to handle the total spectrum of "overuse syndromes" that the distance runner may develop in the course of his or her training and competition.

Despite an acknowledged deficiency in the understanding of injuries peculiar to distance runners, a start is being made, and the disabilities of the distance runners are now being seen for what they are, a combination of three factors:

1. An inherited constitutional inadequacy.
2. An acquired susceptibility due to training.
3. Additional environmental factors related to equipment, nutrition, rest, life style, drugs, and the like.

MUSCULOSKELETAL SYSTEM

The injury problems of the distance runner come from overuse. Although any system can be involved, the musculoskeletal system is most often affected in overuse syndromes among distance runners. More specifically, the musculoskeletal problems are a result of the following, either singularly or in combination.

1. Structural instability of the foot or low back.
2. Muscular imbalance of strength and/or inflexibility.
3. Leg-length discrepancy.

Biomechanically weak feet, tight achilles tendon, tight calf muscles (gastrocnemius and soleus), hamstrings, and quadriceps account for the majority of foot, leg, and knee injuries. These include metatarsalgia (pain along the tops of the feet), heel-spur syndrome, achilles tendonitis, shin splints, posterior-tibial tendonitis, stress fractures of metatarsals (long bones in the feet that extend to the toes) and fibula (the smaller lower leg bone), chondromalacia patella (runner's knee), and the like.

Tight, inflexible posterior muscles, weak abdominals, and leg-length discrepancies account for the majority of low back, hip, and sciatic nerve problems. Furthermore, muscle pulls occur in weak or inflexible muscles; hamstring pulls occur where the quadriceps (front thigh) / hamstring (rear thigh) strength ratio is unbalanced. Adductor pulls (muscles high on the inside of the thigh) occur for similar reasons.

Emerson once said, "There is a crack in everything God made." The distance runner is no exception.

During an ordinary one hour training run, a distance runner averages over 5000 strikes on each foot. This not only searches out congenital structural defects in the runner's musculoskeletal system but also introduces additional stress factors. These congenital and acquired postural problems are often accompanied by those imposed by the runner's foot gear, the surface on which he or she runs, and the training schedule.

Runners may also be afflicted with symptoms referable to the chest (hidden asthma and the "stitch"), kidney (recurrent blood in the urine), gastrointestinal tract (intermittent diarrhea), or to some preexisting disease like diabetes, peptic ulcer, migraine, or sinusitis.

Still, overuse of the foot, leg, knee, and low back constitute the major source of disability in the distance runner. It is a misnomer to think that injuries of these areas are due to the overuse itself. Overuse is simply the precipitating factor. Runners almost always have a weak foot that is structurally inadequate for the stress of long distance running. In addition, their training schedule progressively overdevelops their posterior muscles of the calf, hamstring, and iliopsoas at the expense of their shins, quadriceps, and abdominal muscles. Furthermore, their shoes and habit of running on roads where the crest pronates the uppermost foot contribute to demands on an already overstressed weak foot, The need for a habitual flexibility program as an injury-prevention factor is a must.

An injured distance runner should first have the diagnosis established. Each overuse problem needs thorough investigation; otherwise the identical problem will recur, thereby restricting or terminating the athlete's career. This is not usually difficult in the foot, leg, and knee; however, the entire foot-leg area must be viewed as a continuum so that proper weight bearing of the foot is accompanied by daily stretching of posterior leg muscles and strengthening of anterior muscles.

The clinical picture of stress fractures of the metatarsal, plantar fasciitis, heel spur, achilles tendonitis, shin splints, and the like, is most often a simple matter. In almost every instance of knee pain, chondromalacia patella or tendonitis is present. However, sciatic syndromes and adductor pull can cause difficulty. Sciatic irritation can cause pain anywhere, from the buttock to the big toe, and it often causes numbness of the foot during long runs. Adductor pain is also a seldom diagnosed, intractable problem.

Once the diagnosis is established, the patient should be examined for any structural defects in the foot, leg, or low back. The primary and most important defects are in the foot. Any pronatory (turning outward of the sole of the foot) influence can cause trouble, but the most prevalent one is Morton's foot.

Morton's foot, sometimes called an atavistic foot, has ultimately one result—faulty weight bearing on the first metatarsal segment. In the classic Morton's foot, there is a short, first metatarsal (long foot bone leading to the big toe) and a long, second metatarsal. The sesamoids (tiny bones at the base of the big toe) are displaced posteriorly. Finally, there is hypermobility of the first metatarsal. X rays of the Morton's foot disclose all of these abnormalities plus a hypertrophied second metatarsal. This last satisfies Wolf's law that, as a bone's function changes so does its structure. This long, second metatarsal, which has to take more than its share of the initial foot strike, is peculiarily susceptible to stress fractures.

Morton's foot is present in about 33 percent of the population, but 80 percent of patient population have the short, big toe/long, second toe configuration. The remaining 20 percent probably have the hypermobile first or other more subtle pronatory problems.

X rays will also reveal many minor but significant abnormalities of the lumbosacral spines when runners are plagued with sciatic problems. Dr. Allan Ryan has shown the importance of thorough X-ray examination of this area, and he has stressed the importance of oblique films.

Some physicians use X ray to check out leg-length discrepancy although observations of the standing patient with the hips at eye level is a simpler and more accurate test. A carpenter's level placed over the knees of a patient, seated with feet flat on the floor, will often show a one-quarter to one-half inch discrepancy. This difference is usually shorter on the left and may result from pronation of that foot.

The examination should then proceed to strength-flexibility evaluation. Training does three things to a distance runner's muscles, and two of them are bad. The prime movers, the gastrocnemius, the soleus, the hamstrings, and the ileopsoas (muscles that cross the front of the hip and lift the thigh) become tight and inflexible. Simultaneously, the antagonists, the shin muscles, the quadriceps, and the abdominal muscles become relatively weak. The runner should be evaluated for tightness of the posterior muscles, and their range of motion should be established. Testing of the anterior group for strength will almost always show significant weakness. Muscle testing will also indicate the precise location of the pain and indicate the injured muscle group. The presence of excessive lordosis (forward curviture of the lower back) is presumptive evidence of a tight, powerful psoas, with the invariable accompaniment of weak abdominals.

Examination, diagnosis, and treatment cannot be carried out by the runners themselves, and it is obvious that the injured runner must be able to consult knowledgeable medical personnel. Fortunately, more physicians are being made aware of runners' problems and, with the assistance of the athletes and their coaches, will become increasingly useful in dealing with runners' injuries.

Finally, the physician, the coach, and the runners should acquaint themselves with the runners' shoes, their training schedule, and the surfaces they use. All of these are important in the production and prevention of injury.

Running shoes range from good to terrible. Some are no more than gloves. They lack support, shank, shock absorption, heel counter, and they have very little heel. Each brand, however, puts out an acceptable training shoe. These have a wedge-shaped heel shank with a multilayered sole and a good heel counter. Shoes such as Puma 9190, Adidas, SL-72, New Balance 380, Nike, or Tiger Cortez all have these necessary features. However, none have enough support for major biomechanical problems in the foot.

These problems are accentuated by running on roads, the usual training site for most distance runners. The crown of the road supinates the lowermost foot, which is all to the good, but it pronates or flattens the uppermost foot thus aggrivating any preexisting problems.

So there you have it. Distance runners bring to their sport basic weaknesses that are further aggravated by the effects of their training, shoes, and the surface on which they train. Each injury that they sustain is the product of these factors interacting. Rarely will any runner be treated successfully when one of these factors is unrecognized or ignored. Treatment, just as is the case for diagnosis, must be total. In all musculoskeletal disease, the object is to restore structural and postural balance. This is achieved through supports or exercises. Drugs, whirlpools, cortisone shots, casts and surgery, and acupuncture do not get to the cause and therefore have little place in the treatment. Rest, or a layoff from training, may sometimes be necessary if proper preventive measures have not been employed; however, rest itself cannot be considered a cure for the cause of the injury.

Every athlete, whether injured or not, should be on maximum flexibility exercises for posterior muscles and on strengthening exercises for anterior muscles. Figures 15 to 25, on the following pages, give examples of exercises that deal with most of the problems faced by runners.

The exercises must be done for about ten minutes before and after training every day. Since a runner's muscle problems increase rather than decrease with training, exercises are a daily necessity.

The syndromes arising from the foot-leg area can be divided into three groups.

1. *Those Affecting the Foot Itself.* These include stress fracture of the metatarsal, metatarsalgia, plantar fascitis, and heel spur. In these cases, we will almost always see the genetic factor (Morton's foot) accompanied by a tight calf muscle. Treatment must be directed to the entire foot, as well as to the muscular imbalance. Although the problem seems localized to the heel or metatarsal area, the entire foot is failing. The heel must be stabilized, and the hypermobile first metatarsal must be supported. Stretching exercises must be done for calf and hamstrings.

2. *Those Affecting the Guy Ropes Supporting the Foot.* With achilles tendonitis, posterior tibial tendonitis, and shin splints, the foot is often at fault. The imbalance in strength and flexibility is an added and, sometimes, as in shin splints, a decisive factor. Therefore, the foot must be treated, as well as exercises added, especially stretching for the calf and strengthening of the anterior chamber group.

3. *Those Affecting the Joints of Skeletal System.* Chief among these syndromes, and the most frequent injury to distance runners, is chondromalacia patella, an irritation of the back of the knee cap. Chondromalacia represents a typical pain syndrome while running, going up hills, walking up stairs, or after arising from a chair. Again, this is due to pronation of the foot and subsequent torque or twisting of the leg on the thigh. The patella then rides out of its groove. The Morton's foot is found in most cases, as well as tight calf muscles and hamstrings.

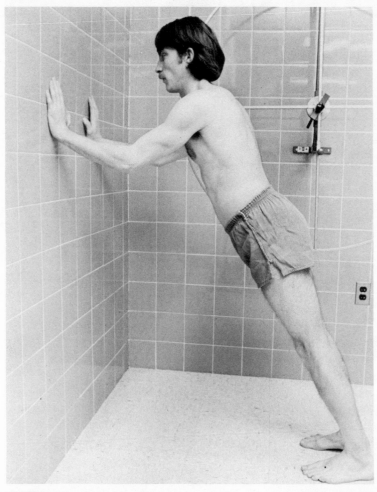

FIGURE 15. Stretching the gastrocnemius and soleus (calf muscles).

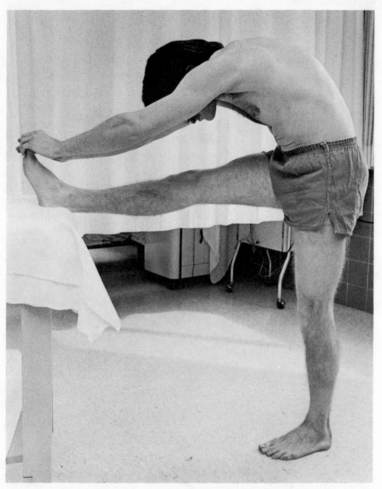

FIGURE 16. Stretching the hamstring muscles (back of upper leg).

FIGURE 17. Stretching the adductor muscle (inside thigh).

FIGURE 18. Stretching the iliopsoas (upper front and inside of hip-thigh area).

FIGURE 19. Stretching the back muscles.

FIGURE 20. Stretching of back muscles, hamstrings, and calf muscles.

78

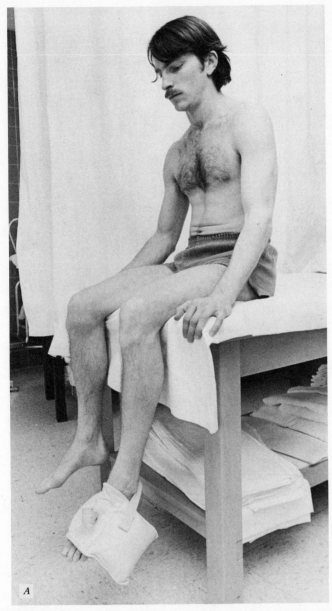

FIGURE 21. Strengthening the anterior chamber muscles, position
(*A*) at rest.

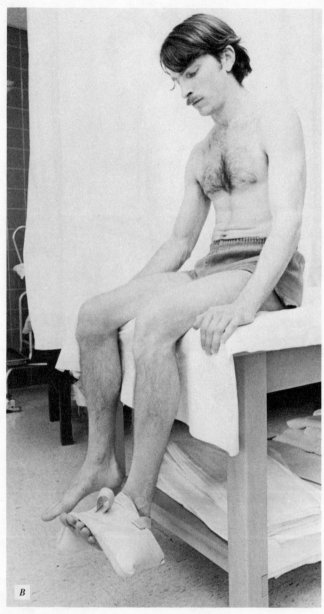

FIGURE 21. (*B*) Dorsiflexion (upper flexion) of the foot.

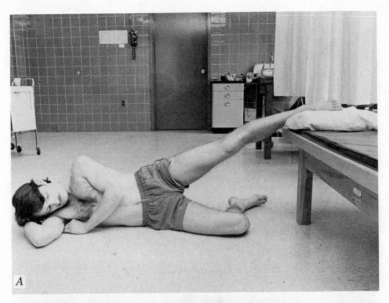

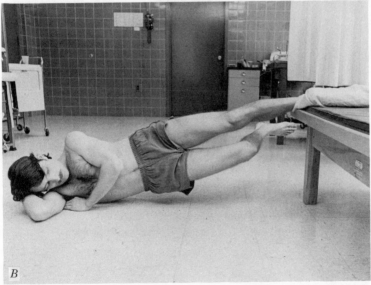

FIGURE 22. Strengthening the adductors, position (A) at rest, (B) suspending body weight.

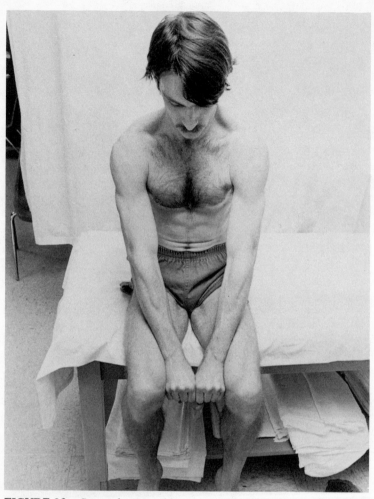

FIGURE 23. Strengthening adductors.

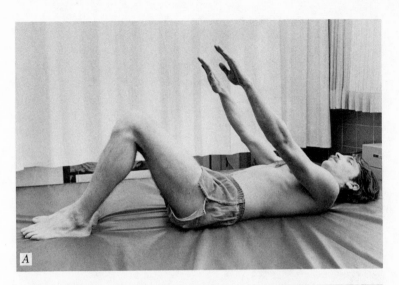

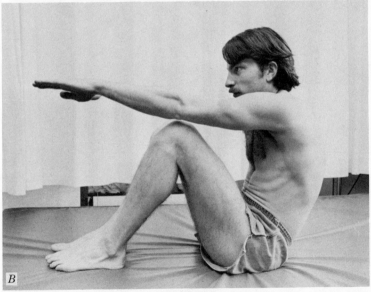

FIGURE 24. Strengthening abdominals, position (*A*) at rest, (*B*) flexion of the trunk on the leg.

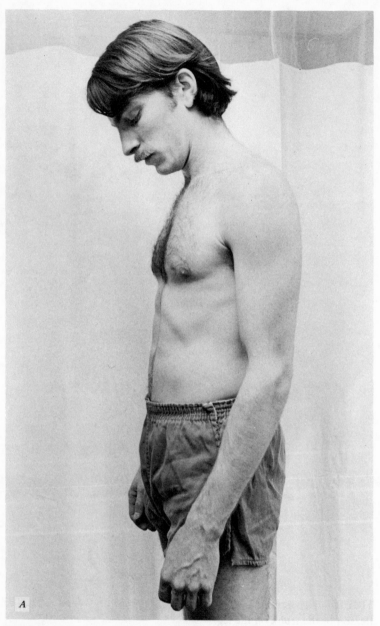

FIGURE 25. Strengthening the abdominals, position (*A*) at rest.

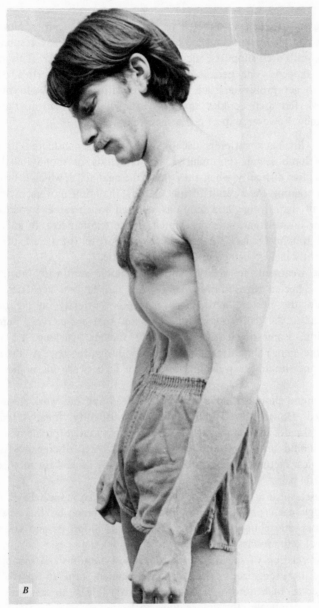

FIGURE 25. (*B*) Isometric tightening of the abdominals.

Treatment, then, is directed to these specific difficulties. Morton's foot or other biomechanical weaknesses of the foot may respond to Dr. Scholl's arch supports, such as "610" or "Athletic A". This sometimes happens: one person buys eye glasses in Woolworth's, others have to get professional advice. So it is with runners. Do-it-yourself surgical, felt arch cookies and heel lifts sometimes can do the job. Generally, however, expert podiatric care is needed.

The low-back sufferers usually have what is considered to be a minor lumbosacral abnormality, a spondylosis or spondylolisthesis. This causes difficulty when they reach the next stage, which is brought on by training. As a result of this training, the prime movers, including the calf, hamstrings, and iliopsoas, shorten which causes hyperextension or lordosis and puts the stretch on the sciatic nerve. In addition, speed training causes further hyperextension in the thrust off and frequently makes such conditions symptomatic.

The treatment for sciatic syndromes should start with the use of negative-heeled shoes during daily work and daytime activities. This corrects the posture and alligns the spine correctly on the pelvis.

Next is the daily use of the exercises that are pictured here. In addition, isometric six-second tummy tucking (sucking the navel into the spine) should be done regularly during the day. At the same time one should grasp an imaginary coin in between his or her buttocks.

Training should be at a slow pace; speed and hill work should be avoided. Downhills exaggerate the back difficulty. Finally, training shoes should have adequate heels. Any associated problem in the foot should be corrected. Occasionally, leg-length discrepancy is the etiological factor in this disorder and should be looked for in all cases of sciatic pain.

Muscle testing and exercise prescription is also a specialized field, although each physician should be able to prescribe the essential exercises—stretching of gastrocs, hamstrings, iliopsoas, and strengthening of shin muscles, adductors, and abdominal muscles.

The relation of speed training to sciatic symptoms and shin splints should be recognized. When distance runners turn to speed, they exaggerate their lordosis, and their forward lean stresses the shin muscles; practically, this comes down to:

1. Support of the feet, starting with adequate training shoes and adding devices to stabilize the heel, elevate the arch, and correct weight bearing.

2. Corrective exercises for inflexibility and weakness.

3. Changing direction on roads or track when necessary.

4. Abstaining from speed work when necessary.

Taking some typical problems at different levels, we can analyze the mechanism and outline the treatment.

1. Heel spur, right foot, in a 55-year-old distance runner. Patient has Morton's foot, tight gastrocs and hamstrings, complains of heel pain, and tight calf area. He or she runs against traffic and wears Puma 9190; recently added speed work and switched to no-shank shoes.

ANALYSIS. Morton's foot puts strain on plantar fascia, which anchors at heel spur. Tight gastroc puts further strain through midfoot as the runner comes over foot strike. Speed and no-shank shoes finally blew the fuse.

TREATMENT. Arch support with heel lift, stretching exercises. Return to training shoes, stop speed work temporarily or reverse direction of track; run with traffic on roads.

For reasons not yet clear, in another runner the same primary situation will cause trouble in the guy ropes that support the foot, the achilles or the shin muscles, or the posterior tibial tendon, which forms a sling under the foot.

With a third runner, the foot and leg will be spared. Instead, these factors will transmit a twist or torque to the knee. When this happens, the patella rides out of its groove over on the condyle, and the cartilage on its undersurface becomes irritated and degenerates.

2. A 50-year-old distance runner with pain in right buttock and thigh. Patient has Morton's foot, tight gastrocs, hamstrings and iliopsoas. His abdominals are weak and lordosis is present. X rays show 1° spondylolisthesis (forward shift or slipping in lower back vertebrae). Foot X rays show short, first metatarsals, long hypertrophied second metatarsal.

ANALYSIS. Pronation of foot plus inflexible muscles exaggerate lordosis and traction on sciatic nerve. Weak abdominals are key to hyperextension, and spondylolisthesis makes this clinically significant.

TREATMENT. Strengthening the abdomen (bent leg situps) and stretching the posterior muscles and wearing negative-heel shoes at work will rotate the hips backward and flatten the spine. A small sacral belt (Sacrogard) may be helpful. Pronation of the foot should be corrected. Leg-length discrepancy should also be corrected.

Again, the foot and muscle imbalance contribute to a back problem to which runners are predisposed (their back X rays tell us that).

Prevention or treatment of overuse syndromes in runners will not be successful unless all of these factors are considered. Symptomatic treatment that is aimed at the effect rather than the cause will end in frustration for both the athletes and their physician.

Unfortunately, the physician often tries to handle these complex problems without the aid of other essential health-science professionals like podiatrists, physiotherapists, and osteopaths. Indeed, at this stage, trainers, coaches, and even athletes themselves are at times more knowledgeable than those who are certified in the field.

The best person to direct this therapy is someone who is an athlete and is in general practice or internal medicine. He or she will be able to integrate this care, calling on the various specialities to do what is necessary. Otherwise, the runners are likely to get captured by a specialist, and they will not receive needed help in other areas. Few runners will respond to less than total care. The primary-care, physician-athlete should be the athlete's ombudsman.

BLOOD IN THE URINE

Blood in the urine is one of the worst things that can happen to a distance runner. Actually, it should be described as pigmenturia, since the color may be due to:

1. Hematuria.
2. Hemoglobinuria.
3. Myoglobinuria.

The runner should make every effort to get an immediate urinary specimen and have it examined as soon as possible. Differentiation of these three disorders is the most important part of the diagnosis. Unfortunately, subsequent specimens are usually normal.

Hematuria. Blood in the urine is a phenomenon that is yet unexplained. An initial, complete urological survey including cystoscopy and intravenous pyelograms should be performed to rule out some coincident process. Only rarely will any pathology be discovered. Renal biopsies in such athletes have shown no significant disease. A report in the Japanese literature of decreased clotting because of exercise requires more study.

Hemoglobinuria. This disorder occurs because of a breakdown of red cells in the body. It may be due to foot impact. The suggested treatment: better shock absorbent shoes plus Spenco inserts. Use grass or dirt surfaces for training. The condition tends to be cyclic and there may be some autoimmune or allergic problems.

Myoglobinuria. It is due to breakdown of the muscles. Again, some people are susceptible, and the condition may be precipitated by ultralong distance, heat, or dehydration. Extreme changes in diet may also create this disorder. Some runners have already learned to avoid carbohydrate-loading techniques because of cramps. Possibly, this may be a result of undiagnosed muscle breakdown that is not yet visible as myoglobinuria.

GASTROINTESTINAL SYSTEM

Running stimulates peristalsis and creates some difficulty in the gastrointestinal tract. Runners should have a bowel movement before training and races. Otherwise they are likely to experience pain or cramps, or diarrhea during or after their running. This may be particularly evident if they have colitis, a previous bowel resection, or diverticulitis. The use of a low residue diet plus fiber supplied by psyllium seed products can be helpful. Tea should be used instead of coffee, and citrus fruits or anything that could cause an acting gastrocolic reflex should be avoided.

A major problem for some runners is lactase deficiency and a consequent inability to handle milk and some milk products. Yogurt seems acceptable in many instances, however. When diarrhea occurs with special preevent meals, milk should be considered the culprit, unless something else is implicated. For this reason, it is best for the athlete to avoid any special diets prior to competition unless he or she has first experimented with them in practice.

Since runners are vagotonic, they frequently have ulcers or hyperacidity. These difficulties are not a result of the running and may even be minimized by more equanimity and serenity, which comes from the running.

When ulcers fail to heal, I have found two major factors. First, patients who never drank milk, and take it, with the notion that it is the best possible food for the stomach (nonmilk drinkers will make their ulcer worse if they drink milk). The second, and probably the most important factor, is failing to control night secretion. Long acting anticholinergics in sufficient dosage to control symptoms should be used.

Occasionally a runner will have epigastric pain while running. A daricon tablet taken about an hour before the race will usually erase this difficulty.

RESPIRATORY SYSTEM

The main respiratory complaint is the "Stitch." It is a spasm or charley horse of the diaphragm, It occurs for two reasons:

1. Backward breathing.
2. Air trapping.

Faulty use of the diaphragm in breathing and excessive trapping of air causes the diaphragm to stretch sideways and finally go into tetany. Correct belly breathing plus exhalation against resistance will reverse these two factors and prevent a stitch or get rid of it when it comes.

Attention to this type of breathing, a type that might be best taught by a singing teacher, will allow the asthmatic to become a runner. We know that asthma patients can swim without too much difficulty, and we realize now that this is because of the natural, abdominal breathing of swimmers and their exhalation against resistance.

HEMATOLOGICAL SYSTEM

Training causes a pseudoanemia in the distance runner. Brotherhood has shown that the endurance athlete has an increase of over 20 percent in both blood volume and in hemoglobin. Unfortunately, for the observer and also the athlete, the blood volume increases slightly more, and therefore the finger stick hemoglobin would lead the examiner to believe there is an anemia present. Actually, the athlete has a quart more blood than the spectator and does not need any iron or vitamin supplements.

CARDIOVASCULAR SYSTEM

The main cardiac complaint of the runner is palpitation or irregular pulse. The main abnormal finding is usually in the EKG. There, an examiner may find any of the three principle changes.

1. Rhythm disturbances varying from Wolff-Parkinson-White syndromes to first and second degree heart block.

2. Repolarization anomalies with T-wave inversions in almost any lead.

3. Hypertrophy, usually of the right overlead type.

Such changes along with the athlete's bradycardia are the result of training and an increase in autonomic tone, particularly of the vagus. No treatment is necessary. The main requirement for the examiner is to use these tests to study athletes, not to screen them. He or she must realize that well-trained athletes have EKG's that are normal for them and abnormal for anyone else. We cannot, therefore, inflict our ignorance on these runners and keep them from their sport.

Studies by Morganroth have shown that there is a definite endurance athlete's heart. It has a larger diastolic volume but no increase in the ventricular wall; the ejection volume is, of course, increased. This heart is not abnormal, simply a bigger and better one.

STALENESS OR OVERTRAINING

Runners who are at their peak are a razor's edge from going over into an area where they are totally inefficient—where when they reach back for that extra effort, it is not there and their competitive times precipitously deteriorate. This is know as staleness and should be guarded against at all costs. There are some who say that such a state is inevitable and will occur regularly during the year, and nothing can be done but to accept it. The state of staleness is evidently one of exhaustion, an exhaustion that affects a person both physiologically and psychologically. It usually follows the introduction of speed training—for instance, fast interval runs—or it comes about after extensive, competitive efforts. In general, it is signaled by such symptoms as loss of appetite, fatigue, loss of attention span, sore throat, swollen glands, depression, insomnia (usually awakening repeatedly during the night) elevation of pulse, nervousness or irritability, low-grade muscle or joint pain.

As you can see, these symptoms are vague and nonspecific and can occur from time to time to anyone. There is no good, early warning system for staleness. Runners have to be on the alert for it. They should incorporate prevention measures such as a routine day off a week, alternating hard-easy days, early naps, and increasing sleep to forestall its arrival. Once it comes, no therapy beyond cessation of activity for a period of time, three days to two weeks, seems to help. During that time, I advise taking a nap at the time runners would ordinarily train. When the day arrives when runners can look on the prospect of running with zest, they are usually clear of the staleness period.

Pulse rates taken in bed, on awakening, may tell you if you have recovered from yesterday's training. A pulse rise of ten beats would advise you to skip that day's workout or, at least, take it very lightly. For the most part, a runner has to be aware that a peak performance usually is a warning to drop off a little in training. Pursuing further improvement with more work is frequently destructive, as so many runners have discovered.

It is best to follow the distum of Bill Bowerman: A bad race in 95 percent of the cases means that one has overtrained. Training should be arranged to lead to peak performance not more than two or three times a year. Once peak time is reached, the runner should back off and cut down, particularly on interval training and racing, the two most stressful parts of the runner's program.

SECTION 7
Profile of Champions

To the casual observer, few champion athletes are less impressive in a noncompetitive setting than are champion distance runners. As a group, they appear undernourished and weak; puny might best describe the general appearance of the highly trained distance runner. The longer the distance for which they train, the less impressive they seem to appear.

The fact is, most distance runners are weak, at least in terms of strength activities. This is particularly true if a distance runner is compared with an athlete trained for almost any other sport, where strength is a major factor.

However, rated on a different scale, one which measures cardiovascular, respiratory, and metabolic fitness, or the ability to endure adversity in the environment, the champion distance runner is a wonder. Few athletes can measure up to the physiological fitness attained by endurance runners; few need to.

Just what are the desirable physical and physiological characteristics of champion distance runners? This is what we will now explore. In addition, some consideration will be given to how the champion distance runner acquired these characteristics and how long he or she might expect to maintain these desirable attributes.

93

BODY BUILD

From a standpoint of body build, the most obvious characteristic is leanness. There does not seem to be an ideal height; we have seen and still see champions who are short, medium, and tall. Because of the rather wide variation in height, there is also a fairly broad range in body weight. The ratio of weight to height does not vary much, and if body weight (in kilograms) is divided by height (in centimeters), the ratio for top male distance runners will usually fall between .33 and .39; female distance champions will usually have a little lower ratio (.31 to .33). Young runners often fall well below .30, showing a lack of muscle mass relative to overall height.

Unlike many other endurance sports (rowing, swimming, cycling, for example), distance runners must support their body weight against the pull of gravity; this work against gravity continues throughout the entire period of a race, with no rest or recovery phase as can be expected on a downhill stretch of a cycle race or at each turn of a swimming race. The continuous support of body weight and the demands of maintaining a fast, running speed combine to make the most desirable body one that presents the least possible weight for the energy producing systems to provide for. Thus the good distance runner is lean. Successful male distance runners invariably carry less than 8 percent body fat and many carry 5 percent or less. Female distance runners have generally been thought to be less lean than their male counterparts, and in fact many do carry over 10 percent body fat; however, it is not uncommon for champion female runners to have less than 10 percent fat and some are in the 6 to 8 percent range, along with the males.

The desirability of a light body weight can be carried too far, however, especially if a lack of muscle mass is a contributing factor. Maximum oxygen consumption is very dependent on muscle mass, and even though $\dot{V}O_2$ maximum expressed in relation to body weight (milliliters per kilogram per minute) correlates far better with distance running ability than does absolute $\dot{V}O_2$ maximum (expressed in milliliters or liters per minute), the former can be overemphasized. It may not be desirable to lose a few pounds so that the ratio of $\dot{V}O_2$ to body weight increases; it would often be more desirable to better train the muscles to be able to handle a greater oxygen supply.

Young (early teenage and younger) runners often are capable of reaching $\dot{V}O_2$ maximum values (expressed in milliliters per kilogram) that are similar to mature, champion distance runners, but they appear to lack the muscle power needed to run as fast as the older runners, relative to the same oxygen consumption in relation to body weight. This can easily be seen in the small weight to height ratio mentioned earlier. The younger runners also often use more oxygen per kilogram body weight to run the same speed as adult runners (more even than less-successful adult runners). The point to be made here is that a light weight-to-height ratio is not the only factor in terms of successful distance running; certainly it should not become the primary concern of the aspiring runner.

Now that we have looked superficially at the distance runner, what less-obvious characteristics might we expect to find?

Basically, distance running ability is limited by (1) the body's maximum energy producing capacity (both aerobic and anaerobic capacities must be considered); (2) the effective use of available energy sources and energy-providing capacities; and (3) adjustment to environmental stresses.

AEROBIC CAPACITY

Possibly the most widely studied characteristic of distance runners is $\dot{V}O_2$ maximum. Indeed, aerobic capacity (milliliters per kilogram per minute) must be high to expect success as a distance runner. However, the range of $\dot{V}O_2$ maximum found among champions is relatively wide (from about 70 milliliters per kilogram to the mid 80s for men and from about 60 milliliters per kilogram to mid 70s for women). On the other hand, success as a distance runner is by no means guaranteed just because a $\dot{V}O_2$ maximum of over 70 can be measured; it may not be realized even with desire and dedication to training. A rather misleading body of data is available that shows all successful distance runners to have high aerobic capacities, and the assumption is that all the people with high aerobic capacities are potentially great distance runners. The misleading fact is that there are people with high $\dot{V}O_2$ maximum values who are not good distance runners; still, this attribute does appear to be a necessity.

Just what contributes to or limits $\dot{V}O_2$ maximum has been discussed earlier; Table 5 summarizes the contributing factors of $\dot{V}O_2$ maximum among champion distance runners as they compare with less well-trained individuals.

To what extent $\dot{V}O_2$ maximum can be increased through train-

TABLE 5. Comparison of champion distance runners and nonrunners on various physiological attributes that may affect $\dot{V}O_2$ maximum.

		$\dot{V}O_2$ max (ml/kg)	HEMOGLOBIN (g %)	MAXIMUM HEART RATE (B/min)	STROKE VOLUME (ml)	CARDIAC OUTPUT (l/min)	MAXIMUM VENTILATION (l/min)
Distance runners	Male	70–85	14–16	180–200	165–220	30–40	160–240
	Female	60–75	12–14	180–200	110–150	20–30	100–150
Untrained adults	Male	40–50	14–16	180–200	110	~ 20	~ 120
	Female	35–42	12–14	180–200	80	~ 15	~ 85

ing has been studied somewhat, but the degree of improvement depends on various factors such as state of fitness and health, and amount of weight that is excess in relation to running weight. To increase $\dot{V}O_2$ maximum by 20 percent is one thing; to increase $\dot{V}O_2$ maximum per kilogram by 20 percent may be quite a different matter. Figure 26 shows some changes in $\dot{V}O_2$ maximum that might be expected with training and a change in body weight.

It does seem obvious that $\dot{V}O_2$ maximum may be changed a certain amount, and that this amount of change is somewhat limited. This further leads to the widely accepted belief that $\dot{V}O_2$ maximum is a characteristic that is quite dependent on heredity; each person is born with a potential $\dot{V}O_2$ maximum that may be partially or completely realized with proper training.

One major genetic factor that most certainly contributes to $\dot{V}O_2$ maximum is the makeup of muscle fiber types of the individual. Successful distance runners have a higher percentage of slow-twitch red fibers than do athletes who stand out in other track and field events. The concentration of oxidative enzymes and mitochondria in the muscles are also known to be greater in successful distance runners.

SUBMAXIMAL OXYGEN CONSUMPTION

Another important characteristic of distance runners is their utilization of oxygen in performing a given workload or running at a given speed. It is becoming more accepted all the time that there are variations in how much oxygen different runners consume while at any submaximal speed. This is often referred to as "efficiency." A more-efficient runner runs at a submaximum (i.e., 6:00 mile) pace at a lower oxygen consumption than does a less-efficient runner. Champion distance runners have a good combination of $\dot{V}O_2$ maximum and efficiency; some have higher maximum values and are not so efficient while others who are more efficient may not have quite as high a maximum. Consequently, both are capable of about equal performance. (Figure 27 gives an example of differences in $\dot{V}O_2$ maximum and efficiency in two equal performers.)

What contributes to good running efficiency is not well known. It might be hypothesized that genetic factors play an important role. It has been shown that there can be some efficiency differences noted in a runner during different levels of running fitness. Whether training

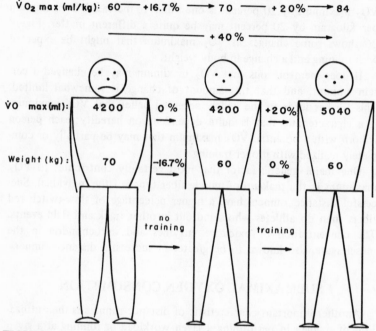

FIGURE 26. Changes in absolute $\dot{V}O_2$ maximum (milliliters per minute) and relative $\dot{V}O_2$ maximum (milliliters per kilogram per minute) that might be expected as a result of training or weight change. (From *Track and Field Quarterly Review*, 74 (3): 149, 1974, Ann Arbor, Mich. 48104, U.S. Track Coaches Assoc., Publishers.)

can be specifically geared toward improving efficiency, as it can be toward increasing aerobic capacity, is not understood.

From the little data available thus far, it appears that female distance runners are as efficient as men, but there tends to be greater variation in this characteristic among women.

Another important characteristic of successful distance runners is that they can perform at a high percentage of their $\dot{V}O_2$ maximum with little or no buildup of lactic acid. They appear to be able to perform relatively greater work (i.e., run relatively faster) for prolonged

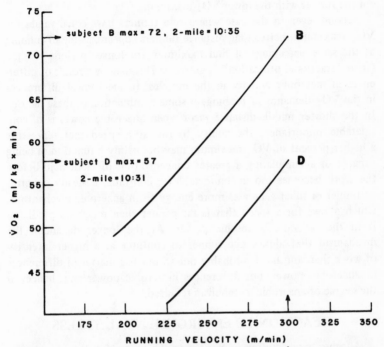

FIGURE 27. Differences in the relationship of $\dot{V}O_2$ and running speed for two runners of equal two-mile time, who have very different values for $\dot{V}O_2$ maximum. (From *Research Quarterly*, **45** (4): 345, Copyright © 1974, Washington, D.C., American Alliance for Health, Physical Education, and Recreation, Publisher.)

periods, without relying much on anaerobic energy-producing processes. Actually, there are two considerations to be made here.

First, since the better distance runner usually has a higher $\dot{V}O_2$ maximum, running at a speed requiring 90 percent of this maximum may demand energy production that is 100 percent or more of another runner's $\dot{V}O_2$ maximum, just because of a lower maximum in the slower runner. Even if both runners can run at 90 percent of their respective $\dot{V}O_2$ maximums with equal comfort, the speeds represented by 90 percent of the two maximums are not the same, and to run at the same speed would demand greater anaerobic involvement, earlier discomfort, and a quicker dropoff from the particular pace for the runner with the lower $\dot{V}O_2$ maximum.

Second, even in the case where two runners have equal values for $\dot{V}O_2$ maximum, better long distance runners appear capable of running at the same percentage of that maximum for longer periods of time (their "fractional utilization" is greater). This may be a result of differences in metabolic activity in the muscles, to mechanical differences in the $\dot{V}O_2$ demands of running, or some combination of these factors. In the shorter middle-distance races when anaerobic power is of considerable importance, the ability to run at a speed that represents a higher percent of $\dot{V}O_2$ maximum may be mainly a function of being capable of accumulating a greater concentration of lactic acid before the work becomes too uncomfortable to continue. Basically, a better half-miler or miler generates more energy from anaerobic mechanisms, which allows for a speed that is far greater than might be predicted from the individual's aerobic power. At the longer distances, the mechanism that allows one runner to continue at a higher intensity of work than another is probably not so much a matter of differences in anaerobic power, but differences in aerobic power and, hence, in the degree of anaerobic metabolism required.

REACTION TO ENVIRONMENTAL STRESS

Another consideration in comparing the successful distance runners with those who enjoy less success, is reaction to environmental conditions. Basically we are talking about temperature, altitude, and training.

Just as there are differences in the desirable reactions to different types of training, different individuals can react differently to changes in the environment. Certainly, we know that a runner from a cold climate will have trouble keeping up with a heat-acclimatized runner in a distance race on a very hot day. The same thing applies when a sea-level runner races an altitude-acclimatized runner in a race at altitude.

The differences between two runners who are normally equal performers may not be so great as in the above examples, but if the two race on a hot day, their individual reactions to the heat may not be the same, with the result that the environment has allowed one runner to be better under these conditions.

Probably the major consideration in this context is that heat, cold, and altitude (as is true of training and detraining) affect an individual's capacity for, or reaction to, work on a *relative* basis; that is, work capacity may be lowered 16 percent or improved 12 percent, etc. Given the fact that successful runners have greater work capacities than less successful runners, and that both benefit by training to the same relative degree, it is easy to see that the absolute additions to an already existing capacity or reaction leaves the better runner still better off than the athlete who has less to begin with.

AGE AND EXPERIENCE

A discussion of distance runners would not be complete without some mention of age and years of experience. Even given the genetic potential, opportunities for training and competing, and desirable motivation, a great distance runner will not emerge in a few months. One may make a real breakthrough in performance and achieve international stature in a brief period of time, but training of some kind certainly took place for a more prolonged period.

First, it appears that real, international success in distance running cannot be expected before maturity. Even with training from a very early age, "open" competition success must wait until at least some time in the late teens. Whether a certain number of years of training is required before maximum potential is reached is not known. With proper training, aerobic capacity can be improved over a period of several years, but an individual's potential is to some extent limited by age. If aerobic training begins early in life, there is probably a better chance for a greater improvement than if it is started in middle age. Physiologically, the best distance running ability should be reached in the middle twenties, but champions can be found who are both younger and older. These atypical champions most likely have very outstanding potential, and proper opportunities and motivation came at an age other than the most ideal one. Still, they could succeed in spite of this slight handicap because of a greater-than-normal potential.

It is extremely difficult to put a limit on the duration of years over which a champion might expect to find success. A runner who has extremely high potential may win without ever tapping the limits that really exist; with advancing age, harder training and more motivation may allow this runner to continue winning through a more complete realization of the existing inherent ability. Another runner, who gains success only through a complete utilization of all physiological attributes, may find continued success not possible as the limits of vital systems start to diminish. Therefore, one runner may enjoy a relatively short period of great running, while another may win for 8 or 10 years or more.

The same possibilities exist relative to optimum age. Factors other than purely physiological ones may prevent optimum performance during the years of greatest physiological capabilities. Even though an individual is not putting the most ideal combination of factors together, success can still be realized if the factors that are combined represent better performance capacity than can be put together by other competitors in the same event. In other words, there are ideal combinations of factors that contribute to success in distance running; the best combination may never be realized by many runners. However, often a less-than-optimum combination may be good enough to allow success; no one really knows how much a performance might have been improved if everything had fallen into place in an ideal way.

INDEX